Going Bananas
My Trailing Career
(Volume 1)

Going Bananas
My Trailing Career
(Volume 1)
Pauline Isabel Dowling

MÒR MEDIA LIMITED

Going Bananas

My Trailing Career

(Volume 1)

Copyright © 2017 Pauline Isabel Dowling

Photograph of MV *Avelona Star* © Fotoflite, supplied by kind permission of Fotoflite

ISBN 978-0-9954874-6-8

First published 2017

Mòr Media Limited
Argyll, Scotland

www.mormedia.co.uk

Cover artwork by Gill Bridle
Design by Helen Crossan, with assistance from Rachel Crossan Hopkins

DEDICATION

To my husband, Captain Stuart MacCormick Ross (H),
for making near-death experiences great fun.

CONTENTS

PHOTOGRAPHS

ACKNOWLEDGEMENTS

Many thanks to Captain Stuart MacCormick Ross (H), whose advanced husbanding skills offered me a brand new previously unimagined trailing career. Thanks to Jennifer Allan for her careful reading. To Gill Bridle for the artwork and particular thanks to Helen Crossan of Mòr Media whose advanced design and editing skills enabled me to come out as a trailer.

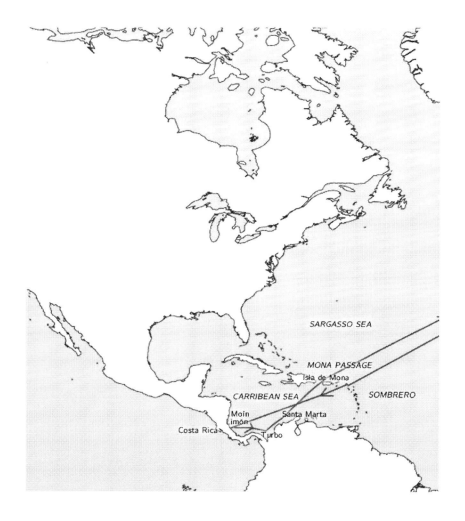

SARGASSO SEA

MONA PASSAGE

Isla de Mona

CARRIBEAN SEA

SOMBRERO

Moín
Limón

Santa Marta

Costa Rica

Turbo

1 The Voyage of the

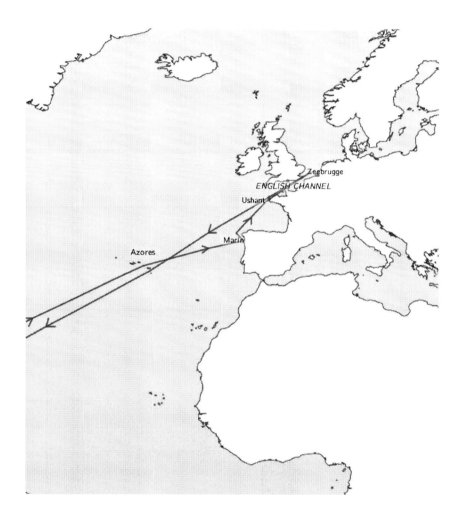

MV *Avelona Star*

SEPARATION

I'm sick of it now
Thoroughly – heartily – sick of it

Sick of seeing your eyes brim, your face crumple,
and your pain trudging up the path

Sick of seeing two blue suitcases stuffed and carted away

Sick of trying not to imagine it weeks ahead

Sick of the foreboding intimacy the night before

Sick of this overpowering
socked in the guts
will I ever breathe normally again listlessness

Sick of the
He'll be back soon
It'll fly
At least you've got him
And all the other cricket bat clichés
Slogging my sadness to the far horizons

But most of all

I'm sick of writing it down

2 MV *Avelona Star*
© *Fotoflite*
The MV *Avelona Star* was built at Smith's Dock Co Ltd in Middlesbrough, to a
design by Akers of Norway. It is an "A" class, fully refrigerated, five-hatch cargo
ship, fitted with banana doors. It was launched on 12 May 1975.

ZEEBRUGGE

It's freezing in Zeebrugge. Sheets of icy rain are swirling about the ship, hammering the water, and sweeping across the dock. As befits my station, I glide from our Mercedes taxi and am almost disrobed by a vicious gust. There's no one around. Then, just as we are about to step onto the dangerously swinging gangway, someone shouts and waves at us to stop. In the ensuing melee two shivering, half-dead stowaways are bundled off the ship by a posse of purse-lipped Belgian policemen and a couple of slavering dogs. As they stumble past, I offer their hollow eyes a sympathetic but meaningless smile. It's no use to them of course, but I can't let them pass as though we humans are not all fundamentally connected. Neither can I see misfortune as a mere spectacle that makes travelling so colourful. Of course, I'm not condoning drug smuggling, but this is nothing to do with drugs. They have gambled: taken the equivalent of a lottery ticket and paid with their lives. They have submitted themselves to two weeks on a violent ocean in a pitch-black freezing hatch, on the off chance they will be alive enough at journey's end to collect their $20,000. Of course, anyone who knows anything about banana boats knows that they don't just carry bananas; I have even heard it said that bananas are a simple distraction. But I know nothing about that, and care less. What I do know is that with these drugs come real humans, and some die long before they reach Europe. But knowing it is one thing. Looking into the faces of the truly desperate at the mercy of the profoundly greedy, is quite another. It is not a good start and I hope not an omen.

At the top of the gangway, by contrast, the well-fed Filipino crew are all smiles. Wrapped up like mummies in balaclavas, scarves, gloves and huge coats, they shake our hands enthusiastically. Two run down and come back with our luggage and by the time we get to the suite it is there.

At first sight, the master's suite looks more dosshouse than luxury pad. In the dayroom, the settee's loose covers are ripped, the blue blinds have been patched with swathes of silver tape more normally used to hold engine room pipes together, and one window has been replaced by a sheet of badly painted steel, beneath which a huge very old television and video are bolted to the wall. Neither work, but beside them a bashed about radio lights up and gurgles in Flemish when I accidentally kick it.

'I remember when the *Avelona* was new,' H says. He was an officer trainee (a cadet with a degree) when the British Merchant Navy—and the Blue Star Line in particular—was at its zenith and, unbeknown to career advisors, about to start its spectacular slide and take him with it. After a while, he says, 'I can remember the first time I stood in here. I just couldn't believe captains lived in so much luxury.'

'Luxury!' I snort. Going to work with my husband or—as I call it—trailing has encouraged snorting. 'This must be the original stuff, then.' I rub my hand over the heavy, faded Sanderson linen, the blowsy floral much favoured by ship-owners and aspiring or arrived toffs, wondering how on earth we are going to make this home, why we are expected to, and whether the Vesteys would put up with it for four days let alone four months. Or even whether they care enough to know what state their ships are in.

'At least we're getting a new mattress,' H says, in a transparent attempt to cheer me up. I lift my laptop onto the huge polished desk but when I pull out the original, good quality office chair, the back collapses and a castor falls off and rolls around the deck. I could snort, but don't.

From the window, I look down on three gaping hatches totally covered by bright yellow waterproof towers which balloon at the bottom into huge skirts. Inside, a spiral conveyor is twisting its way to the top, connecting with a covered track above the dock that takes the bananas straight to the shed. A procession of cardboard boxes is rattling up all three spirals continuously.

3 Working spiral conveyor

Deep in the hatches, stevedores are loading the belts. From time to time, they come up on deck and urinate against the ship's side, the luminous stripes on their red jackets glowing in the ship's lights. Some whistle and gaze about nonchalantly and many have single earrings, blonde permed hair with optional ponytails, and look as though they are only stevedoring until some disc jockey recognises the market value of their demo tape.

'Nobody likes being in Zeebrugge,' the chief engineer tells me at dinner. 'You never get any peace. If it's not the office people, it's surveyors, or suppliers, or chancers tramping all over the ship.' And sure enough, as we sit in our formal gear, our attempt at refinement and ceremony is mocked by a constant procession saying 'Captain?' or 'Chief?' and expecting them to jump. 'This simply wouldn't happen on a French ship,' he adds, 'they'd all have to wait. The French are far too respectful of food.' For the next half-hour we all wish we were French.

After dinner, we pad up and run across the freezing dock to the huge, dimly-lit and extremely noisy shed, where banana boxes are running about everywhere. There are 170,000 for discharge and a continuous procession is rolling in through the upper floor and straight under the scrutinising gaze of two burly quality controllers, rather like bouncers, who eye them up meanly and pounce on any they don't like the look of. They are looking for "yellows". Only green bananas are wanted in the markets; yellows are bad news. They spit when they see them.

The greens rattle on, little tracks like demented miniature railways, going in all directions towards one of the automatic pallet stacking stations where box after box is piling up, ready for the forklift trucks. From time to time, what appears to be a madman screams up, plunges his fork under the box mountain and careers off blindly and recklessly towards a line of waiting trucks or a cool store. To avoid being gored, run over, or both, we scuttle along the authorised path under large signs warning against deviating. We know not to get between a green and its destiny.

At the other end of the shed, the quality controllers are down at the mouth. They have many yellows and they point (it is too noisy to speak) at a great stack of discarded boxes, looking as though they might be going to puke.

'Whose fault's that?' I ask H, as they seem to be blaming him.

'There's always some,' he says unmoved, 'but it's only a minute fraction of the number we carry. What really matters is that we get most of them off the ship as green and cloned-looking as the day they were loaded, without complaints from the shippers, hefty insurance claims, or human disasters.'

So that's why we're here. His job description. Sounds simple enough.

Next morning H disappears early, muttering about finding more blankets and getting a new mattress. We've hardly slept, partly because we were freezing and partly because every time we turned over, broken bedsprings pinged like violin strings. When I finally crawl out, the first thing I see is my goose pimpled body dissected by more engine room tape, this time holding the mirror together. To warm up, I run a bath. The water is scalding (good) but a hideous red colour (bad), a cross between an ancient Egyptian beauty treatment and the contents of an old radiator. Afterwards I looked like a table-ready lobster. But I am warm.

By the time I am a suitable colour for breakfast, the saloon is deserted until, that is, a large ungainly stranger lumbers in and sizes the place up as though looking for somewhere to hide. He half looks at me, registers thin air and grunts as he sits down. 'Did you have a good trip?' I ask brightly, in my role as Captain's perk, i.e. someone with advanced and universal relating skills. Whoever he is, and wherever he has come from, he didn't. After a slight pause, he looks at me savagely and says, 'We are all in the hands of God.' I say nothing, which is all the encouragement he needs to launch into a diatribe about God being the creator of everything, while shovelling in Shredded Wheat as though God has ordered it and it is a trial.

'It's all there,' he says between mouthfuls, 'it's all there in the Bible. And … it's all true.' I'm not sure whether I have done something to provoke this, so smile in a glacial way. 'Quite frankly,' he goes on, which is an introduction which encourages snorting, but I desist. 'Quite frankly, I get mad as hell with these evolutionists. Mad as hell.'

'Really?' I chirp, wondering why he has chosen this moment and my presence to start unravelling. He softens at what he takes to be interest.

'The Bible is quite clear. Heaven is out for anyone who does not take Jesus into his heart.' This man has more than a bee in his bonnet; he is raving and at sea you learn to humour any sign of deranging, so I smile less glacially. 'And I'll tell you what,' he says as though I'm the lucky one, 'there is no way round it. Heaven is real and, well, I don't fancy the other place.' He smiles and chuckles. Satanically.

Despite his urgent need for an anger management course, his manners are excellent, and when the steward asks would he like his eggs sunny side up, he nods absently and says we are all sinners, every Jack man one of us, which I think rather appropriate. Adherents can be dangerous. For a while, he is content to deal with his fry-up, and then suddenly he jumps up mid-sausage and says it has been lovely to meet me, he has enjoyed our conversation, but he has just remembered …

Naturally, this leaves me mentally exhausted and thinking what hard work it is being a perk.

My unexpected trailing career began in my flat in West Hampstead, London when I decided I wanted to take a ship to New Zealand. Because my father had died, I had been back and forward to New Zealand, making sure that my mother was as comfortable as possible. I simply could not face another 30-hour ordeal trying to sleep sitting up and all the other well-documented inhumanities that long haul flights entail.

The idea was inspired, I thought, but as it was before cruise and freighter travel became common, I had no idea how to make it happen. Initially local travel agents looked mystified, but eventually I found one in London and was offered a berth on a Polish or a British ship. I opted for a Blue Star Line container ship travelling from Tilbury to Auckland. It was several times the price of flying.

The journey should have taken four weeks but the ship, romantically called the *ACT 7*, lost its steering gear in Botany Bay and we ended up tied up in Darling Harbour with Sydney at my door for almost three months. And for much of that time, I was the only female on board. So now I trail. It's as simple as that. The details are not important, except to us, and all I will say in my defence is that the mating cry of the lone seafarer was very siren indeed, and any woman walking up a gangway should be advised that a single man at sea (of which there are or were many) is not only in search of a wife, but he may well be rather desperate. And of course we are the slaves of our genes, unless we tie ourselves to the mast and plug up our ears. I did not do this. I listened, and I liked what I heard.

Because my passage coincided with the only dockers' strike for some time, the ship didn't call at Tilbury and I had to be ferried to Rotterdam. On the same day, H joined the ship, having been flown there from another ship to replace the chief officer. The fates lined us up.

So now I go about the world—not according to my will, but where I am taken—like a breathing, talking parcel. Challenged daily to be dignified, sane and fulfilled. It's a strange life, not without its merits and not without interest. But I will leave you to decide that. And I may even tell you something about this man I married who in due course became a captain. The man I call H, which is short for husband, a quite beautiful word I never dreamed I would be able to apply with total accuracy.

4 Leaving Zeebrugge bascule bridge up

The day is a uniform grey as our engines start and we ease away from the fruit berth in the inner harbour. The dock sheds are all shut up and the great unloading towers are silent, their voluminous yellow skirts hanging limply in the damp air. On the dock ahead, there are several hillocks of coal, and the flatlands all around are dotted with petrochemical chimneys and the occasional line of spindly birch. The wind has dropped and, round the edges where the dull sky falls to earth, the greyness grows woollier.

I love this moment; wherever I am, no matter (almost) how grotty or oily the harbour may be, those first moments when the ship and the dock begin to part touch me in a way all partings should but few manage. Trains, planes, cars are all parting disasters, tearing and awkward or worse—over in a flash. But ships get it right. As we slip from the berth, centimetre by centimetre, those parting emotions—hope, sadness, excitement, fear—rise up and quiver on the edge of flooding in a fine balance that is poignant, romantic and full of possibilities, yet not overwhelming. I fall for this every time. I long to throw streamers and sing.

As the gap widens and we edge into the midstream, the lone figure of the agent on the dock slowly shrinks, while up forward and down aft the crew shiver in as many clothes as they can wear and still work the ropes. Once clear of the berth they leap about to keep warm as we head towards the Pierre Vandamme lock. Ahead a huge mass of steel, the four-laned coastal road, is slowly rising and when it is high in the sky and the lock doors have slid into their inner chambers, the tugs pull us in and the mooring gangs in thick padded anoraks tie us up.

Near the lock, patches of dead-looking grass are thick with oystercatchers. Some are poking about with their long bright red beaks, others are suddenly running a few steps on their short legs as though they have just thought of some urgent business and just as quickly forgotten it, and the rest are standing about, looking pretty. Before the development of the port of Zeebrugge, the wild and windswept dunes of this part of Belgium were covered in shorebirds. I close my eyes and imagine it.

This sea lock, which was completed in the mid-eighties, is 500 metres long, 57 metres wide and with a usable depth of 18.5 metres, if that helps you visualise it. The sliding doors (there are two sets at each end) and the rising bascule bridges are so magnificent, they should win the Turner prize. And the fact that they have had to divert two canals—the Schipdonk and the Leopold—by means of sluices and culverts and other feats of engineering, just adds to the wonders. And the result of all this unsung but amazing engineering is that Zeebrugge now has two harbours: an outer, serving roll-on roll-off (ro-ro) ferries, container and cruise ships, and the inner two basins, which are deep enough for general cargo, bulk carriers, and the procession of fruit ships which land an uninterrupted supply of bananas, citrus, and tropical exotic fruits which are not only cheap, considering the cost of transport alone, but allow us to ignore seasons and historic eating habits, and to be so alienated from the source, we can grow up thinking food comes from supermarkets until, that is, some crisis threatens the supply.

The Port of Zeebrugge has an interesting if chequered history: it is only in the last few decades that it has finally been developed, yet it was more than a century ago that Brugge began to plan for an outlet to the sea for their pretty city which would put it back on the international trading map. Brugge is Europe's most beautiful backwater because it snoozed through the industrial revolution, and even when it woke up and wanted a share in the burgeoning North Sea trade, it was almost too late. Holland and France already had most of it. To make matters worse, the burgers squabbled for decades about where the outlet should be, seeing it only as the first stop on a canal which would carry ships of any size to Brugge's important doorsteps, giving them a pivotal place in world trade and hauling them into the twentieth-century in one move.

When they finally managed to agree on a plan and inaugurated it in 1905, there was dancing in the streets for a week, the whole town kicking up their heels and licking their lips at the thought of the tidal wave of riches which would eventually wash up the expanded canal. Which was uncharacteristically abandoned for the Flemish apparently, and a bit misplaced because, hardly were they up and running when the Germans invaded and turned Zeebrugge into a such a successful submarine base that they wiped out more than half the allied and neutral shipping fleet, before laying waste to it all when they left. The resistance stopped this happening in the Second World War, but there is terrible ruination from which the whole area is still recovering and which partly accounts for it looking so featureless and unprepossessing today.

The pilots change in the lock; the docking one leaves and one of the deep sea Wandelaar pilots, whose headquarters is a launch about an hour down the coast, boards. The two pilot system is quite rare now. Docking pilots, who were once common all over the world, are now considered an expensive irrelevance. And here there is 'feeling' between them. The

Wandelaar pilots could do the whole job, but the docking pilots are hanging on to their sinecure.

The Wandelaar pilot is long, thin and fit-looking, with a runner's physique. He has a kind face and a distinctive way with esses. 'Your shstowaways captain, they have made you famoush. Your sship has been on TV last night.' This is news to H, who smiles the smile of one keen to know more without betraying his complete ignorance. As mentioned, our cabin TV doesn't work. 'I wonder how many come and are not caught? Security is not so good in Zeebrugge. Anyone can walk off these ships and into our country. It is not the first time for these two, apparently, and now they will have a very nice holiday.' He chuckles happily. Belgians are not obsessed with the seriousness of international drug trafficking, let alone their part in its continuing success. 'Our Belgian prisons are very comfortable. Better than their homes I'm sure. Televisions, saunas, gyms. They won't want to be free.' More chuckles. There may be truth in this, but I've heard Britain's squalid, Victorian, overcrowded, slopping out dumps called holiday camps, and they're such fun that inmates regularly kill themselves.

But it certainly is—or was—true that Zeebrugge lacks security. Many stowaways come confident of success and equipped with maps of the docks, tools, walkie-talkies and some even have stevedore's uniforms. What's more, despite their terrible ordeal, some make repeat trips, which is why ship-owners have been pressing the port authorities to tighten things up. No one wants to carry stowaways; it's hard enough delivering perfect greens without frozen unfortunates amongst them.

Eventually the road starts to rise and the lock gates slide home. 'Bridge to forward—let go the spring line,' says H into his walkie-talkie.

'Forward to bridge—spring line clear,' crackles the second officer (who's up forward).

'Bridge to aft—let go the stern line,' H again, and the *Sea Lion* tugs us out.

'Dead schlow ahead,' calls the pilot.

'Dead slow ahead,' repeats the chief officer and we pass under the huge vertical road into the outer harbour and towards the long grey breakwaters where enough windmills are turning in the wind off the North Sea to power the whole dock complex. 'Unfortunately,' says the pilot, 'the authorities say this electricity has a virus so they can't sell it to the National Grid, no matter how much the wind blows in Zeebrugge,' and chuckling he walks towards the bridge wing with H in tow and calls, 'Steady on 342!'

'Steady on 342!' booms the AB (able-bodied seaman) at the wheel immediately and a few seconds later, 'steady on 342 now, Sir,' and his voice ricochets off the bulkheads, projected and resonant enough to be heard on either bridge wing in any weather. The wheelman has to be operatic; confirming we're on course is a vital job.

'Bridge to forward—let go the tugs,' says H.

'Stop engines!' calls the pilot and a few seconds later, 'dead slow ahead!' and the tugs buzz away, leaving us set fair for the breakwaters.

They are not pretty things, these jumbled heaps of concrete cubes which sweep their long arms in a secure embrace round Zeebrugge, but they keep the pounding North Sea out and, like the lock, they are at the highly impressive end of the engineering scale. Beneath the surface layer upon layer supports the massive blocks each one of which, the pilot tells me, weighs 20 tonnes. Even the sand at the very base had to be replaced granule by granule with less porous stuff as, for many years, Zeebrugge had a serious silting up problem.

'Half ahead!' calls the pilot as we near the turreted stone of the original and prettier breakwater they call the Mole, from where the radar tower and traffic signal mast flash messages. The *Cristoforo Colombo* (a dredger) is coming in as we pass into the North Sea and not far behind that a P&O ferry.

To starboard, the new breakwaters stretch north to the rolling sands of Heist and Knokke. To port, the coast is low until Blankenberge's clumpy seafront apartments appear, looking like a row of upended bricks. It's busy, but visibility is good and by the time the pilot cutter comes into view, things are calm on the bridge and in the water, and the little wooden cutter has no trouble making a lee. 'I'm off now, Captain,' says the pilot, and he shakes all our hands, 'Keep her hard to port; she's coming nicely like that. Safe journey, and perhaps we will see you again. And off he goes behind the chief officer, down the stairs to the pilot ladder on main deck.

'Pilot away, 14.55,' says H picking up the binoculars and scanning the horizon. 'Starboard 272!'

'Steady on 272!' calls the wheelman and we're off to Costa Rica.

Visibility is good as we head for the Dover Strait, and at four o'clock, when the chief officer's watch starts, H comes down for a rest. But he can't relax. Whenever I speak, he stares intently as though he is lip reading, which is supposed to make me think he is gripped, and to mask the unmaskable fact that he is listening to every extraneous noise and monitoring every slight course deviation. Also, he's up and down every few minutes, checking the forward-facing windows and saying at least there's no fog. These are some of the world's busiest waters, with massive ocean-going vessels, ferries, pleasure craft, fishing boats and possibly people in baths to look out for (although probably not swimmers at this time of year). Add to that a healthy proportion of incompetent watch keepers, who think the radar is a video game, plus old tonnage which should have been scrapped years ago, and it's dangerous enough without fog.

H stays on the bridge till midnight: the third officer can't be left in busy waters, but I don't resist our new mattress for long.

5 Captain Ross on the bridge with the pilot and the wheelman

6 Captain Ross in his office

THE CHANNEL

Just after 0100 hours the phone goes. We are approaching The Casquets, the traffic separation scheme near Jersey and, whatever the weather, H has to be on the bridge. I stir briefly, but sleep again and the next thing I know it's 4 am and a fully-dressed person is getting into the bed which is lurching about like a bucking bronco. 'I've told the chief officer to call me if this gets any worse,' he says, as I feel a wool and polyester mixture leg creeping tentatively towards mine. 'It's better if I keep my clothes on in case....' he says apologetically as though, in my frenzied lust, I may tear them off.

'In case what?'

'In case I have to get up there in a hurry.'

'Is it going to get any worse?' I try to sound light-hearted, and suddenly we are both almost tipped onto the deck first to one side and then the other as the ship pitches, corkscrews (a sort of mid-air dance) and then bounces several times, slamming down so thunderously the vessel screams. There are ominous clatterings in the dayroom, so I get up and grope about putting movables where I think they'll be flung and tipping chairs upside down.

'I don't like this,' I say, as calmly as possible. 'I know banana boats roll. Everyone who's ever been on one has gone on and on about the rolling ("oh aye they roll (lass), if you think this is rolling let me tell you, you don't know rolling till you've been on a banana boat."), but nobody mentioned that they pitched, corkscrewed, pounded and reduced you to whimpering pulp.'

'This is unusual,' H says in his most reassuring tone. 'Especially here. We're not in the deep water yet. But,' he doubles the reassurance, 'we're not in any danger.' All the same, he grabs my hand and hangs on to it as though we are in our joint last moments. 'It's worse because we're heading into it and the ship's empty.'

'What about the onions and the cars?' We're carrying Dutch onions and BMW cars to Colombia. I haven't seen them, but someone said I should pop down to number one hatch and stroke them or perhaps covet them (there's been a bit of both about), but I'm not tempted.

'There's not enough of them to make a difference. Any bad weather and we'll feel it, and really bad, and we'll ...'

'We'll what?' I must know the worst. The very worst.

'It could get uncomfortable.' H is the master of understatement and thinks this is really spelling it out. We try to sleep, but every time there's a big one our eyes open and we roll about together as though practising formation coupling for the sex Olympics. 'This is exciting,' I say icily, as we lurch in perfect synchronisation. I'm not proud of myself.

At first light, we are somewhere near Land's End and pitching so badly that it feels not as though we are in the teeth of a gale but that we are being eaten alive and spat out. H has had no sleep since we sailed, and is back on the bridge permanently, and we're doing 16 knots, which is slow for us, but any faster and we hit the water and bounce about like a ball with no air. The noise is horrible. And the ship could be damaged.

In the dayroom, I tie down all the furniture, jam the fruit bowl, kettle and breakables down the back of the settee and go to breakfast determined to carry on as though being hurled against furniture and bulkheads or walking about clinging to fixtures is normal. From time to time during the morning, BBC Radio 3 booms a bit of a string quartet or effete chat through the bashed-up receiver, reminding me, as I lurch about unpacking and trying to make a home, that we have not gone far and that there are those for whom the floor does not forever move.

The suite has lots of drawer and wardrobe spaces, which is good, but even better, the last captain has left no relics of his personal hygiene regime. Normally I have to dispose of at least the shampoo dregs, the prickly heat powder or sometimes the remnants of the foot sprays they either couldn't bear or be bothered to bin.

Mid-morning I bring up my breakfast—cereal toast and coffee—and soon afterwards the electrician calls to fix the lights in the ceiling, on the desk and the corner table, and to investigate the television. The intimate wall lights still work, but intimate lights are not good to read by, and we need all the lighting we can get to counteract the steel window.

The electrician is a Croatian from Riječka and knows how to suffer publicly. 'This weather terrible,' he says dramatically. 'Impossible to sleep and impossible to work.' I sympathise, but manage—just—not to apologise for it. 'Never mind,' he says, lifting his shoulders as though to shrug off the gloom he is wearing like an overcoat, 'I try,' and he raises his arms and eyebrows, smiles wanly, and starts to poke about in the television.

Meanwhile, I wobble about behind the big desk shuffling papers—I can't concentrate round workmen—telling him I'm not fussy about the in-cabin entertainment but I am about the lights. 'Do you come often with Captain?' He is questioning my sanity.

'Once a year, in the winter.' When he looks surprised, I add, 'This is my first time in the North Atlantic and my first banana boat.'

'Your first banana boat? And your last, maybe?' I decide that is not some sort of Croatian saw.

As we leave the channel and meet the Atlantic head-on, it gets worse. H slows to six knots and spends every second on the bridge, and when I pull myself up the narrow polished stairs and haul open the heavy door, he's glued to the wheel, his screwed-up eyes, bloodshot from lack of sleep, transfixed by the boiling ocean.

I offer to make coffee, but he doesn't feel much like it, which is just as well, as I can hardly stand upright and I certainly can't bear the sight of those over-used eyes or what look like grey, snow-topped mountains hurling themselves at us from all directions. This sea is very confused. Sometimes, between the mountains, a great valley appears and, like a cork or a toy, we roll into it so far that coming up seems impossible.

Yet I know we have lashings of stability, far more than those comfortable container ships in the benign Pacific, which only occasionally let you know you're at sea. H has told me time and again that we could roll sixty degrees and still come up. Reefer ships are famous for surviving seas other boats, e.g. container ships, bulk carriers and cruisers, I'm afraid, disappear in. They are the design of choice for the true survivor. But knowing all this doesn't help; there is always that horrifying moment of stillness at the bottom of any roll, when we could go either away and when I imagine flailing around in the post-capsizing mayhem waiting to be a shark feast. Or, when the bow flies up like a rearing horse and we are suspended in mid-air and I imagine the hull smashing down and breaking in two, forcing me to wonder whether my bit will float, how long I will take to drown and whether I will be with H and what our last words will be. I could be trapped in an air pocket and have time to write my life story before I passed out, let alone drowned.

Even though I do not utter a word about my morbid imaginings, H tells me again we are in no danger, and that at this speed the bow won't bounce about on the waves. He is watching every wave and altering to avoid the most vicious. But in bad weather at sea, if you're not on the payroll, there's not a lot you can usefully do except imagine your end. And at heart I am a realist with pessimistic tendencies. I make intelligent, sometimes exhaustive but, I like to think, this side of clinical, assessments of the possibilities. I know I am only a collection of functioning cells, of which I am very fond admittedly, and that fate cares not a jot for me, and in a second I could be history, wherever I am. The difference is that, on land, I can stay sane by forgetting that for long periods, while on a banana boat it seems I never can.

In one of H's rare visits to the cabin he tells me it is a force 9 whose teeth we are in, but it feels worse because it is straight ahead and there are two swells coming at us at once. 'But there's no danger,' he says for the umpteenth time. 'None at all.'

'Then why are you looking so worried?'

'It's the speed. If we don't speed up soon we won't make our ETA.' With fruit boats, or any delicate cargo, ETAs (estimated times of arrival) are tyrants. The charterer has taken the ship because it can zip across the Atlantic at a reliable 20 knots and collect the freshly-picked and -packed greens on schedule. It's tight, and if the ship is late and the berth missed there are penalties, and somebody has to take the blame so they can sort out who has to pay. That somebody could just be H. His job is to get there and back in time, whatever the weather, and regardless of the cost to his health.

The problem with terrible weather is that it takes over and just getting through it becomes all there is. For a while, I try and experience being hurled about as thrilling, and when that fails I wonder if I will embrace some paradise-touting religion before the day is out. Once or twice I look out to see if there has been any change in my fear levels, and am utterly appalled to see fishing boats on the crests of mountainous waves, and when I see them disappearing into troughs I understand what the true price of fish is.

At this point my mind begins to let go of naked fear and I see at last that things could be worse: I could be on that fishing boat, in a yacht, or even in the lifeboat. This thought is so horrible that I realise my fear is not of death but of either being a) eaten by sharks, or b) cast adrift in that open boat (the ship's too old to have the new covered comfy-looking ones) and having to perform all my bodily functions in front of people I hardly know, while freezing, wet, and so dehydrated I am ignobly tempted to scoff more than my share of the drinking water rather than nobly resorting to my own urine.

When H comes down for dinner, after the chief officer has eaten and is back on the bridge, he is looking remarkably awake and in control apart, that is, from those bright red eyes. After dinner, we sit together in the dayroom like strangers waiting in a bus shelter for the rain to stop, saying (politely) these loose covers could do with a stitch and wishing we'd bought the Scrabble even though the tiles would be all over the floor and I'd be incapable of any word which wasn't capsize or shark.

Every now and again one of us says, 'I'm sure it's calming down; it's ages since the last big one' and H mentions barometers, isobars and the latest forecast and how good the dayroom is looking already even though we're sitting on the kettle, the iron, cups, and books and all the chairs are upside down.

Because we don't know what else to do, and we want to distract ourselves and have no means of doing so, we try, without success, to play the video of our Scottish island home, Lismore, which a friend made to make H's lone sea passages seem less lone. It featured me in lovely September sunshine supposedly doing typical island things, e.g. coming off the ferry or strolling about our croft among the wild flowers and doe-eyed bullocks with a glittering Sound of Mull in the background, and ending with a huge orange fireball dropping below the Morvern hills and a full moon rising over Appin. It is very scenic, but it too rolls and the horizontal hold button is useless.

'How would you like to go to the Royal Garden Party?' says H, fast-flipping through the company magazine and clutching at straws. I stare. He must know by now that there are places to which even I will not trail.

'Why?'

'A picture here,' and he shows me one of the masters in full Merchant Navy regalia, and his partner, who look as though they could be in amateur dramatics, but are in fact standing proudly outside the palace.

'I think I'd rather be here.' We both snort. 'What about you? Would you jump at the chance?' I'm too concerned with my mortality to really care, but in normal life the idea that I had married someone who would ever ask me to trail to a Royal Garden Party (except for the copy/irony), would be alarming. And I don't think the company would like to be represented ironically.

'Well, I thought …' but what he thought I will never know, because he stops, turns ashen, and rushes for the bridge. Seconds later the bow is out of the water, I'm thrown to the floor and the ship seems to be vertical. Left alone, my heart in my throat choking me, I grab the loose covers, tear them some more, and wait horrified and breathless for our noisy, terrifying, violently bouncing landing.

THE ATLANTIC

I appear to have survived: I might even have slept a little. H spent most of the night up top (as they call the bridge) while I lie face down clinging to the mattress by my fingernails, trying to stop myself being thrown in the air like a rag doll or hurled to the deck. As far as this indifferent and cacophonous ocean is concerned, we are no more than a cork or one of those fish farm boxes I often see from my window being hurled senselessly towards the shore. And unfortunately, I also know we are at the mercy of twenty-year-old iron and steel.

When I first went to sea and knew nothing of rupturing tanks and ageing steel, far from being afraid, I almost relished the occasional battering in the Bay of Biscay or even the Great Australian Bight, where a gigantic swell marches up unimpeded from Antarctica and thrashes the land. But then I was in love with the sea. In love with the vastness, the roundness and, most of all, the emptiness. It was a world swept clear of clutter (the pollution, alas, is not seen) and I no longer had to sort out what mattered in life's constantly growing heaps of dross. Quite unexpectedly, I'd discovered a context where my inner reality matched my outer.

In those innocent days, I listened incredulously to people saying the sea was boring and I certainly never understood the excitement when we passed another ship, miles from anywhere, let alone the euphoria when we saw land. Whales and birds, yes; ships and land, no. To me, ports were never shopping opportunities, but places I had to put up with until I was deep sea again, steeped in the peace of an organic art gallery offering constantly changing textures, patterns, light and colours. But best of all, I loved the feeling of travelling over the earth at a speed I could keep up with and not being hurled violently through time zones.

But then, on my first trip, I was a single passenger on the *ACT 7*, a large, comfortable container ship. I had no responsibilities, no idea of the dangers, pretty good weather, a gym, a library, a pool and my hardest job was sitting at the captain's table selecting from the huge, delicious, no expense spared menu. It was all far removed from banana boats in the winter Atlantic, sailing under a foreign flag, downsizing to near extinction, and dodgy tonnage.

7 The *ACT 7* in Wellington

In its day, the MV *ACT 7* had been impressive and still was when I sailed on it. What it lacked in aesthetic appeal it made up for with utilitarian solid reliability. It was one of the largest container ships in the world when it was completed in Germany in 1977. Working ships being things of great beauty disappeared after the war, although cruise ships have always attempted to look appealing. However, the officer accommodation on the *ACT 7*, while not grand, was roomy and pleasantly comfortable, and I have sailed in both the chief officer's cabin and a tourist cabin, which was in fact a converted cadet cabin. I never saw the crew accommodation. In the early nineties, the *ACT 7* was sold to P&O and became the MV *Palliser*

Bay, but as the flagship of Blue Star Line it sailed from Tilbury to Australia and New Zealand returning and round Cape Horn via Lisbon to Tilbury. A very pleasant world cruise indeed.

I'm relieved to see daylight, not that there's any improvement, just more to think about, e.g. throwing up, being flung against bulkheads, and hit by wardrobe doors. But as these are now normal, I decide to get on with it. After breakfast, I set my laptop up on the big desk in the dayroom, bear hug it with one arm so it doesn't lunge towards the deck, jam my knees under the desk, turn the chair wheels so they don't roll, and type with my spare hand. Unfortunately, every time I look up, the horizon is going up and down like a mad blind and, when my stomach starts doing the same, I bring up my breakfast. Staring at my ghostly reflection in the bathroom mirror, I wonder if people in supermarkets standing over great mountains of bananas ever wonder how they get there and I'm sick again. Several times.

After what seems hours clutching the toilet bowl and alternately dry retching and whimpering followed by the same lying on the bed, I pick my way down the narrow polished stairs as carefully as a drunk, my laptop in one hand, the rail in the other, and check out first the conference room, which has a huge bolted table and that reverential hush important under-used rooms acquire, and then the spare officer's cabin, which is very private and cosy with a small desk and the bonus attraction of a bed and an *en suite*.

But in neither can I stop the machine from flying off the desk, so I resist the bed and end up in the huge, very public lounge and, by wedging the machine into one armchair and myself into another and jamming the space across the room with furniture, I'm finally secure, if unfit for anything except dozing and self-pity. Behind me, the once posh, now threadbare, salt-encrusted curtains open and close, the glasses hanging in the bar clink and chatter, in the adjoining dining room a chair does the occasional skate about the linoleum, while in the corner of the bar the Christmas tree lights flicker and the fairy on the top sways like a drunk.

'It's always bad until the Azores, but not usually this bad,' the chief tells me at *smoko*. 'For five days we are thrown about and then it's summer. You can count on it.' He should know; he's been on this run for ages. It's 10.30 and everything except watch keeping stops for coffee. The Filipinos are in the duty mess but we *smoko* in the ship's office. Not that anyone smokes, and I am surprised to see that all the calendars are of ships or docks, and one is a rather good seascape which makes a change from naked pouting females dangerously contorting their pelvises in the interest of selling mariners the toughest paint jobs or most exciting tank maintenance. Being at sea can be like moving into your local garage. Mechanics and mariners (some) have a similar need for thrusting pelvises and breasts that appear to be feeding quins.

At lunch, my soup sloshes about, avoiding my spoon and mouth, and my chair keeps skating away from the table because the safety chain is broken. We pour water onto the white cloth to stop things slipping, lie all the sauce bottles down, and use as much energy as we are taking in, gripping the edge of the table.

The officers' dining room is huge. There are still several tables, as though any minute the place will fill up again, but most are never used as only the chief engineer and the chief officer sit down to lunch with H and self. The other officers take it in the duty mess and the ratings mess downstairs near the galley. This means that the steward Juan is up and down steep stairs, plates of food precariously balanced in one hand and hanging on to the rail with the other. Sadly for him and for us (and for the nation), the galley boys have gone, the whirr of the dumb waiter is silent, and it will never be fixed because it is obsolete, and there are simply not enough of us anymore.

Which seems to be a good place to mention that there are twenty-six on board: ten officers, fifteen ratings and me, described on the crew list as a supernumerary. The captain, the chief engineer (known as The Chief) and the chief officer (known as Chief or The Mate) are British, the electrician (the 'lecky') Croatian. The radio officer (known as Sparkie), the second and third deck and engineering officers are Filipino, as are the bosun and his able seamen and ordinary seamen, who work on deck. In the engine room, there is a Filipino oiler and wiper, while the cook and his two stewards are also Filipino and extremely important, as they keep everyone fed and the ship clean.

So far, I don't know any of them, except the tall patrician-looking Juan and the extremely small radio officer who, when he asked for my passport, told me he was a grandfather, and that all his children and grandchildren gave witness to Jehovah. He has a bemused, sickly smile and looks as though he's mislaid his real personality, or it is wrapped in a lot of comforting blankets, so as not to feeling the spiritual cold. In the radio room beside the bridge, he asks if I believe in giving witness, and I say I certainly do which pleases him enormously and his smile spreads to his eyes and almost becomes a wicked chuckle. Almost. We lurch about for a while, discussing the necessity for witnessing. It is not demanding or unpleasant— our spirits have plenty in common and there is no need for specifics. He's wearing his lifejacket, which, I presume, is to do with the weather, but H tells me later it is because he thinks the radio room is radioactive.

'There's a low near Iceland and we're just on the edge of it,' H tells us at dinner, his eyes redder than ever. 'Further north, they are giving force 12 warnings,' which I think is meant to make us feel glad we are not further north. The mate says that he has read somewhere that waves in the North Atlantic have doubled in size in the last fifty years, which is true, but not fit talk, and just then a particularly big one throws the water jug into H's lap and my chair skates across the room. Fortunately I meet Juan before I crash into the opposite wall and have to be winched off for surgery.

'I'll tie you, Ma'am,' he says as I wheel it back, and in no time I am attached to H's chair with thick yellow rope. Our elbows and eyes are dangerously near but, thanks to the storm and the engine, we can't hear each other eating. Eating noises have been the downfall of many a relationship, mine among them. There is a thin line between enthusiastic eating and unconscious chomping. 'There was nothing in my marriage vows about being tied to your chair,' I say, doing my best to appear dignified, despite looking totally institutionalised and not having enough elbow room. H is past letting such things bother him.

One of the ABs has fallen on deck and gashed a hole above his eye, which the second officer has cobbled together with butterfly clips. The second officer is the medical officer, but he can call on H in a crisis. It's years since merchant ships carried a doctor, and then only if there were passengers. Now they keep the number of passengers below the level where the law demands one and, in emergencies, they radio a pool of doctors in Italy for round the clock advice on everything from how to treat a bleeding ulcer, remove teeth or surgically operate. This is a high risk occupation and getting more so; like most senior officers, H has seen people killed and very seriously injured, had near misses himself, and seen others die from natural causes because they were out of reach of emergency treatment. It is not uncommon for a master to have to make life and death decisions, with little more than a first aid course, a well-stocked medical locker, and *The Ship's Captain's Medical Guide* at his side.

Things are looking up. We have had two more hideous days and sleepless nights, but today the sun is out and H is putting the speed back up cautiously, and we are on course again. (We were heading for South Africa at one stage it was so bad). Unfortunately, the swells are still there, the sea is still rushing about like a ferret in a frenzy, and we're doing some mighty rolling. But the wind has dropped a bit, the pitching is decreasing and simple rolling almost feels like a luxury.

Am I giving you any idea of what this is really like? No? Well ... because the floor is so unreliable, you are either walking laboriously uphill and pulling open doors against gravity as though they were made of lead (which some of them are), or you're freewheeling downhill out of control, as though you've been wound up, and flying through doors that open before you, or worse, just close, which means you crash into them and break your nose and/or arm. Just standing on one leg to trouser the other can take a good chunk of the morning and what's left of the day is eaten by small innocuous activities made huge and dangerous. But the worst is the not sleeping or, like last night, being woken many times and getting more and more bag-eyed and slack-jawed and unfit for the day's assaults.

But we all struggle on, both obsessed with the weather and trying to ignore it. And every morning, after breakfast at the unsociable hour of 7.30, I assume I am going to live and wedge myself into the foul weather workstation in the lounge, and write something. Anything. Writing is what I do, wherever I am, and at sea, given reasonable weather, conditions are so good it transforms trailing from tedium to amazing opportunity. Without a mobile occupation I would have given up trailing long ago. Wonderful though H is, following him for months on end, would not be enough much as I like reading, sunbathing, exercising and gazing at him over the Scrabble board. Or even pretending to be interested in bridge, which he has started to teach me.

The copy's good too. And research is just daily life. How else would I know, not just about bananas, but also the unpalatable facts about pirates? In the early days, hand in hand with my love of being at sea, went a naive belief that once we left port we were safe, if not from hurricanes and freak waves, then certainly from attack. Not so. Piracy is as real today as it was when all the great maritime powers were at it, investing their skulduggery with so much myth and romance, that it became the stuff of entertainment, and pirates were rewarded with a knighthood, if they netted enough booty for the sovereign. As a result, the word 'pirate' is now a synonym for exciting, if not brave and daring, and certainly does not describe the reality of being boarded and murdered by thugs. Just as the word 'banana' is innately funny or a synonym for mad, and news commentators cannot help making jokes about the 'banana war', so 'pirate' is thrilling and if you are attacked, the crime will not be taken seriously by anyone.

True, various shipping ministers do from time to time put out notes for the guidance of ship-owners and seafarers, but they give no comfort to those in the firing line, especially as armed robbery with violence is on the increase, both deep sea and in coastal waters.

Sailing in pirate waters is deeply unpleasant, particularly as they are after the ship's safe which is in the master's suite, sometimes at the foot of the marital bed and the deterrents at the master's disposal are risibly inadequate. Time and again, it has been demonstrated that locking all the outside doors at dusk, turning on bright anti-pirate lights and having the ship's hoses ready to wash them over the side should they be spotted, which they seldom are, is no match for those skilled in stealth, who know that there are very few people on today's very big ships, and that most of them are likely to be asleep.

What's more, because there are notices all over the place telling you what to do and not do in the event of an attack, and skulls and crossbones on every outside door, it is impossible to forget where you are, even in bright daylight with miles of visibility and all the crew out on deck. Impossible for me anyway, especially when I was on a ship that had already been done, so was marked as a possible target. Even an easy one.

On that occasion, the unfortunate captain, who had joined that day in Singapore and hadn't even unpacked, came down from the bridge and was standing looking out the forward-facing windows, when several men crept into his dayroom, grabbed him from behind, put a sword to his throat and said (in excellent English), 'Where's the safe, captain? If you don't tell us you will die.' He escaped with his life, which is not always the case, and they got away with several thousand dollars, and nobody knew they had even been until the captain phoned the chief officer to come and untie him.

Pirates know that the captain's safe is full of money, and that they can get it and be away, probably seen by no one. They are certainly not deterred by speed or size; with a grappling iron and rope, they can scale any hull. True, you are more vulnerable at anchor and near the coast, and most attacks occur in the South China Sea, the Melaka Strait, off Brazil, and in parts of Africa. And the very worst of it is that nobody gives a fig. Whole ships can be hijacked and never heard of again, and whole crews lost, and never make the news.

While lack of interest in merchant shipping is not new, complete ignorance of it is. And the reasons: apart from ferries, no one travels routinely by sea, and more and more ports have been moved out of town, while discarded docklands have become shopping venues, offices, or posh flats, which means few people have any idea what a container ship, a reefer, a bulk carrier or a tanker even look like. Then, as goods and food which were once exotic appear in shops routinely, consumers take them for granted and most have little curiosity about who produced them let alone how they got there. In short, the age of the ship as symbol of romance/escape/wealth has gone: Britain no longer builds ships, great cities like Glasgow, Liverpool and London no longer revolve round them, the attendant industries no longer train generations of apprentices, which means that the only ships still in the public imagination are ferries, pleasure craft and cruise ships, which are all closer to being floating shopping malls/hotels than deep sea carthorses of goods and people.

But there is more to it than simple visibility. The Merchant Navy's contribution to British life in both war and peace times has always been shockingly undervalued and under-acknowledged. When Britons think Navy and ruling waves, they are thinking Royal Navy and frigates. Most have absolutely no idea about the huge part the merchant fleet has played in every facet of Britain's becoming one of the richest nations on earth. Let alone their vital role in the world wars, which is why the merchant fleet has been allowed to disappear without a fight, why those who remain are facing dangerously deteriorating conditions, and why pirates are simply getting away with it.

Today—with the improvement—H orders a fire and boat drill, as there has to be one once a week by law. Afterwards we all watch a safety film in the crew bar, a bleak place with poor lighting, uncomfortable black vinyl padded benches, and a lake of dull linoleum. The focal point is an ugly table and a massive TV and video, behind which is a huge poster of a completely naked woman smiling intelligently. It is impossible to ignore her, but fortunately her nipples are more or less normal, and she is not doing anything too dangerous or distracting with a chair. If you didn't know that armies of men were nipple dependent from birth to death, a stint trailing would put you right.

8 Fire and boat drill

I soon wish I'd given the film a miss. Far from comforting me, it fills my morbid imagination with all the ways I could burn to death. The crew stare, eyes wide, mouths agape (when not chewing sweets), as though it is one of their much-loved kung fu blood baths. I wonder if they understand they are being warned, or whether they are gripped by the violence of flames roaring through alleyways when an officer leaves an iron face down on a shirt or drops a lighted cigarette into a bin. Or the suspense when flames lick menacingly about the galley soon after the cook turns the light off for the night, having draped a cloth over a hot plate. And that is without mentioning what oily patches in hot engine rooms can do, or how one tiny careless act can turn the whole ship into a raging inferno before you can say, 'my will's in the filing cabinet'.

In the early evening, we roll past the Azores. In normal circumstances, I would be out on deck with the binoculars, raking the horizon for the lights of São Miguel or Graciosa. But as it's still too rough, I take the odd look out as we pass six miles from São Miguel and 20 north of Santa Maria. Between islands the swell is supposed to decrease, the land interrupting its great oceanic stride for a while at least. It doesn't. There is no change. Not even a hint of a change.

And it's the swell which causes all the really terrifying movement. The sea can be like undulating velvet but, if the swell is hitting you in the right spot, you will be a cork on its lovely surface. Especially in a banana boat.

At bedtime, H gets his clothes off for the first time since we left home. Five minutes later the phone goes. Visibility is deteriorating. The third officer is worried. In a few seconds, the trousers are on again, almost on their own, and H is gone.

When the phone goes at 4am, I am dragged from my first deep sleep. After H has gone to the bridge to speed up, I roll about in the noisy darkness wondering why people pay to do this when, looked at soberly, it is nothing more than an advanced and prolonged form of torture. Yet it is possible to buy a romantic cruise on a working banana boat (with heavy emphasis on the Caribbean and no mention of throwing up or breaking limbs), and while you may be lucky and live, there is also a good chance you will need stress counselling, osteopathy, and a lawyer when you get home. And it's no better in summer. Sure, the Atlantic may or may not be kinder, but in the Caribbean you will be constantly chased or lashed by violent hurricanes with innocuous names.

But we have our distractions. The third officer has been given the job of organising the first of the bingo games. He's selling tickets with a bad grace and clearly thinks himself above organising ship's bingo. Filipino officers (not the ratings) can be prone to throwing their weight about. They seldom fetch or carry anything if there is a rating handy. Reason: they come from one of the top agencies (there are lots in Manila), are well paid, and at home are used to being waited on hand and foot. Bingo is hardly my number one leisure choice either, but, at sea, choice doesn't come into it, and keeping everyone happy is part of H's job, one of the easier parts, especially as most Filipinos love anything that involves chance and winning. At the mere mention of bingo, they beam at H as though he is their guru and he has just uttered.

They also love parties and would celebrate cutting their toenails if they could get away with it, but instead they stick to birthdays, farewells (as their tours are nine months, this is a fit subject), and major religious feasts which merit a mini-fiesta which must include party games with prizes. They are extraordinarily easy to please. Pass the parcel can do more for ship morale than almost anything.

As Christmas is only a few days away, the cook has produced an elaborate programme for the Christmas Eve Fiesta and H is down for Opening Remarks. 'I wonder what they expect me to say?' he says. 'Check the book,' is all I can suggest.

There are two books in the captain's library dealing with how to sail with Filipinos without treading on their cultural corns or making them feel that you hope you'll wake up and find that the British Merchant Navy is still there with flunkies galore and thousands of beautiful ships, instead of a few hundred (and falling) that haven't been flagged-out yet.

Culture Shock, the fatter of the two books, is one of a series written to help ex-pats on land and discusses, among other things, the protocol at christenings, dating etiquette, and how advantageous it is for a girl to have a beauty title. (Imelda Marcos was known as the 'Rose of Tacloban'). The other, *Understanding your Filipino Seaman*, is a quick fix crib of *Culture Shock,* produced in the frantic flagging-out period, of which more later, as a guide to shocked British officers thrown in at the deep end. They are both riveting reads but they have nothing at all about how to open a fiesta. Just rather a lot about how vitally important they are.

The cook is anxious that Christmas dinner be authentic, and has asked me for tips on stuffing and cooking turkeys. Unfortunately, since the army of British cooks left and with them long menus, silver service and saloons full of men in full regalia being served by cummerbund-wearing stewards, I am often asked for my advice on a range of culinary matters. As my interest in cooking has been on the wane for a few decades and my mind now goes strangely blank in the kitchen, the questions always surprise me until I remember yet again that, to some males, female means some vague amalgam of caterer/sex object/emotional prop and sometimes all three.

Because I know that my ideas of a female's role and the cook's meet at no point, it is not easy dealing with the stuffing query. If I say, 'I've never stuffed a turkey in my life,' or, more accurately, 'I have stuffed only one turkey and will never do so again,' that makes so little sense that they ask the question in some other way, or question my sanity or (the very worst) feel so much pity for H that I am in danger of throwing up, and I am doing enough of that already. This time, I get round it by asking what he did and confirming its authenticity and smiling a lot, because I remembered that the book said that smiling is the best way out of a tricky situation (in the Manila traffic, admittedly, but this was near enough).

Filipinos smile a lot, which is just one reason they are agreeable to sail with, especially as these smiles are real and some are beautiful. But smiling is also a vital part of Filipino body language and has a vast range of meanings, e.g. they smile when they mean 'get lost' or 'you are a complete wally but I am too polite to tell you', which strikes me as very evolved in one way, yet it may also account for their country having been occupied so often. And being called after Philip II of Spain.

When the Filipino junior officers and ratings first came in the early nineteen nineties, the British senior officers remaining were convinced they would be sitting down to endless meals of fish heads and semolina, with the occasional tinned peach and evaporated milk. It didn't happen, precisely because Filipinos are extremely adaptable, having been on the receiving end of orders from colonising Spanish and Americans. And most of them are quite capable of producing a decent steak, which is the British seaman's number one passion and the benchmark of a cook's skills. It's early days to know how good this cook is, and they do vary, the best being put to the ships which have passengers, but I already love his soup and his vegetables are nutty and crunchy and his stir-fry delicious with lots of garlic but not too much oil.

I suggest to H, who is a keen cook, that he get the stir-fry secret when things are back to normal. What I actually say is, 'I must eat this on leave. I just must. If we ever go on leave that is,' and he says, 'We're in no danger. We could roll sixty degrees etc.' I don't say it at the table. I know better, because on one ship I burst out with, 'This is divine. You simply must get the recipe,' which is what any partner might say. But several men stopped eating and looked at me as though I had said, 'when we get upstairs I am going to give your gonads a jolly good twist or perhaps remove them altogether', while looking with deep sympathy at H, waiting for him to deliver some crushing blow to his insouciant mate. He laughed, of course, being both amused and perplexed when men rally to his support when he least needs it.

At dinner, I vainly attempt to drag the lecky into the conversation. Otherwise, he just sits there looking like Eeyore and half pie smiling if I look his way. 'English no good,' he says with a smile that is wallowing in resignation. 'I try, I try, I buy tapes, I listen, I sail with British, but these English words,' and he shrugs the shrug of someone who has great shoulder mobility but no ear and says, 'these English, they won't stay in my head. They go in and then straight out,' and he points to his temples to make sure we know the direction and the speed. 'Italiano, that stays, but English, never.'

'What say I were to give you fifty dollars for every phrase that stays,' I suggest.

'Fifty dollars, one hundred dollars, one thousand, they still won't stay,' and his shoulders go up even higher until I can't even see his ears, but he laughs and looks less sad.

After dinner, Juan teeters through the lounge with our coffee on a tin tray with doilies. Huge mugs with lips like boxers wobble about on small saucers. 'The coffee cups, Sir, I look, but they are gone.' Flagged-out probably, we all quip. Still we refuse to give in; we may be all that's left, but there is such a thing as standards. As we struggle to keep them on the coffee table, we show one another photos of our other lives: houses, gardens, crofts, children and pets. It's part of the ship mating process.

Living on a Scottish island and having a croft with bullocks is always good for a bit of mileage, and Lismore always shines in photo sessions. It's beautiful and photogenic of course, and after years of watching the weather on English television, they are all brainwashed into thinking that we in the Highlands are huddling around fires, or going about our business in thermals with our arms folded against the bitter wind, and dealing with rivers of catarrh after every sentence. They think bleak and constant rain and they see sparkling water and me swanning about in shorts and a panama to protect myself against sunstroke. And they gasp. Photos always lie and mine no more than the next person's.

9 Balnagowan looking towards the Broch

10 Our croft, Craignich No 9

11 Ferry at evening: the view from our house

The lecky has new pictures of his son. 'He almost as high as me,' he says excitedly, pointing to above his shoulder, 'and much higher than my wife. She telling me he wear all my cloths and he has 14, one four. Look, this my jacket,' and I see an innocent boy's face on the body of a tall man. He is looking straight at the camera and is beautiful. The lecky is beaming, almost bursting with pride. 'He looks like an angel,' I say, wondering if that phrase will stay.

Outside, the full moon and thick clusters of stars are rolling about the black heavens. 'Clocks again,' someone says. Between Zeebrugge and Costa Rica we have eight hours to add. Not only can we not sleep properly, but every night we have a whole extra sixty minutes to not sleep.

THE SARGASSO SEA

When I first open my eyes, a huge orange moon is leering back at me, the sky is pinging with stars and a swathe of bright gold has been flung across the black water. I have slept all night, the floor is no longer heaving, and the only sound is the dull throb at the ship's heart and the roaring of the cooling fans, both of which are inescapable, in even the most idyllic weather, unless you are high up on the fo'c'sle.

After breakfast, I close the door on the spare officer's cabin, now called my fair weather workstation, and a thick piled peace descends leaving me with no excuse but to write. At home, I can distract myself for hours. Here I am not responsible for the dusting or cooking, so the only distraction, if you can call it that, is the steward's mop pop-popping against the door as he cleans the alleyway. A most agreeable sound.

This was once H's cabin. When he was an officer trainee just out of the University of Glasgow, and I was in London being told by 4D in Bethnal Green that all their teachers had gone 'men'al' and that they would see to it that I did too, H was sleeping in this bed, cleaning himself in this shower and teaching himself French in this armchair (before the arm fell off). As I was losing a stone and suffering terminal fatigue letting 4D know it took more than a few loud-mouthed wide boys to derail my sanity, H was seeing the world. And, he tells me, dreaming of the days when he would be living in luxury in the captain's suite, pottering about with his Meccano or his golf clubs in the mornings, sleeping his afternoons away, while his chief officer and chief steward kept him in touch with the men and made sure he was not disturbed unnecessarily. That only slightly overstates the comfort masters knew in those not very distant days, before owners were told they could greatly increase their profits if they got rid of the expensive, unionised British. They needed only to change the flag under which their vessels sailed, move the whole operation offshore, and get in cheaper labour. They did not say that they would also be jettisoning centuries of British expertise, and seriously overloading the few British senior officers they kept. They called this flagging-out.

While flagging-out is just a phrase now, in the early 1990s it was a tidal wave which swept in and smashed over everything, sweeping British dominance of the sea away and many merchant seamen with it. Flagging-out made mariners feel angry, powerless and not valued, and the government were quite happy to see it happen, offering no help to owners, companies, or seamen. Mrs Thatcher even went so far as to say that if they needed a Merchant Fleet to risk death for them in war times, which she called 'times of national crisis', they would import a cheaper one. Ironically, as recently as 1983, the MV *Avelona Star* was renamed the MV *Castle Peak* and chartered by the MoD to supply troops in the Falklands.

So while other European countries recognised the value of their merchant fleets with subsidies for new ships and so on, British ship-owners painted out the London or Liverpool from their sterns and painted in Nassau or Limassol, and Filipinos, Chinese or whoever were cheap enough were hired, while British officers and ratings went ashore in silent droves. Unlike for the miners and the steel workers, there was no public outcry, no debates and no support groups on picket lines giving them any sort of a send-off. And so the era of accountants who know the bottom line began. Britain had never valued its merchant fleet, just blatantly relied on it to deliver the bulk of its food and goods. And, I should add, slaves to its empire.

Men at sea always feel at the mercy of both managers and unions cosying up to each other in the comfort of their offices, and flagging-out in the 1980s and early 1990s, was easily the grossest example. As a result, the British registry went from 1,640 ships in 1975 to 250 (the majority of which are ferries) and falling. In less than a decade, the skills that had taken centuries to build up were allowed to disappear, while more and more was demanded of the senior officers who remained and who have been struggling ever since with chronic fatigue, and a unique variety of stress, which results from a hugely increased workload. In addition, they must learn to communicate with junior officers with limited English and sometimes limited or even dubious skills and qualifications.

All captains and chief engineers on foreign flagships live with the expectation of disaster; for months on end, they are on a 24-hour watch, trying not to think of the million things that could go wrong, knowing that it is their job, their life, their ticket, that is on the line. When they were all British, it was not heaven and, of course, they moaned and thought themselves undervalued, but the responsibility was shared to a great degree. There is now no sharing. Masters and chiefs can't be everywhere at once round the clock, but if anything seriously goes wrong, they will soon hear the learned judge telling them they should have been.

And with this dramatic rise in responsibility has gone a parallel fall in conditions; less is spent on pay, on accommodation and on their comfort, while vapid rhetoric is all they hear from the unions about the scandalous hours they work. Accountants do not have a column for making them feel valued and no researchers are looking into the effect of sailing up the English Channel all night, discharging all day and sailing down again with perhaps a lie down if they are lucky. While airline pilots, truckers, and even train and bus drivers are having their body clocks monitored, masters and chiefs are delivering the bulk of Britain's food and goods, and hoping they meet their deadlines without hitting anything. Never mind the damage to their biorhythms, immune system and life expectancy.

The ultimate insult is that these same redundant merchant seamen, or their predecessors, had kept Britain fed and many had given their lives in both world wars for which they had received scant gratitude. When 563 merchant vessels were sunk by U-boats in 1940, the British government was forced to introduce food and fuel rationing. And in 1942, when 1322 ships were lost in the Battle of the Atlantic, the need to grow more at home and conserve imported food became vital.

We're in the Sargasso Sea, and rivers of seaweed in swirling lacy loops are galloping by in our bow wave. After lunch, I find a sheltered spot (there's still a cold wind) and sit out, alternately reading *War and Peace* and staring mesmerised at the myriad patterns and endless shades of green and brown seaweed lolloping along. Midships, some of it is thrown clear and dances off in the wavy chevron we are forever creating, while the rest is sucked up by the wake and dances frenetically to the far horizon.

If the weather is good enough, I always sit out after lunch, watching the marbled bow wave and the satiny folds of our wake rolling over and over. It is wonderful to feel the sun and, when *War and Peace* falls, I gaze into the distance and think about Sonya and why no one has ever written a book about her in the way *Wide Sargasso Sea* is about Mrs Rochester. She seems to cry out for a life outside Tolstoy, being a charity child and forever having to feel grateful. When publishers cast around for sequels to this and that, wouldn't you think that Sonya would be a gift? Or is it that she is a Tolstoy creation and Tolstoy is too big for all that. It's all very well to take Bertha Mason out of the attic in *Jane Eyre*, but Jean Rhys only had a Brontë to deal with. Perhaps it would take a mighty nerve to pluck Sonya from Tolstoy. It is the greatest novel ever written. It says so on the back. And it certainly is one of them.

I do not like what Tolstoy has done to Sonya. There is no other character in the novel who seems to have any sympathy for her situation. She appears to exist to be ill-used. As a child, I spent a lot of time being 'parked' (as my parents so accurately called it) with relatives I knew were not entirely thrilled and, naturally, I assumed they personally loathed me. I know why Sonya skirts about the margins, shrinking her natural exuberance and playing the simpering goody-good to Natasha's wildness. So why Tolstoy or anyone should think this bonsai being her true nature is puzzling. Or it would be if shrinking to survive were not universal. Not that it detracts; I could read *War and Peace* forever. A substantial read is a must at sea; there is nowhere else with fewer distractions and the sort of slowly beating time the moneyed classes had when such books were written.

After sunset the sky erupts, the dying light scrawls deep pink randomly all over the sky while darker clouds bubble into bunches of plump chrysanthemums around the horizon, and the racing navy sea reflects it all like a great bruise.

Our first truly exquisite day. The sea looks as though someone has laid a silky throw to the horizon and it is undulating lazily where the brilliant sun strikes it. We glide along, despite doing a fast 19 knots. Everyone's spirits are high and we go about saying, 'This is the life' or 'What a blessing people like bananas'.

In the evening, we decide to watch the film in the officers' lounge. There is one every evening but, because I have an exceptionally low threshold when it comes to tolerating nonsense or even rubbish, and have never grasped the connection between escapist and gripping, I seldom bother with the film. Besides, more than anything, we like to spend our evenings together. And the more we do it, the better we get at it. Nothing beats shutting our doors and pulling the curtains knowing our time is our own, except perhaps the anticipation of it.

We like company too of course, but nothing beats our own. It's even better than solitude, because together it can contain the unalloyed pleasure of solitude. And more than double it.

But at sea, H has to do a certain amount of socialising now that there are so few British. It is part of his job to keep things ticking over pleasantly. Of course, none of this mattered before flagging-out. There was plenty of company for everyone and no one cared or even noticed what 'the old man' did with his evenings. But these nights, there are only one or two in the bar and later in the glow from the officers' video, and everyone's presence counts.

There's not a lot of entertainment at sea these days. Where previously many ships had excellent libraries filled with books and videos people left and the company provided, now videos rule, and the Filipinos want nothing except saccharine karaoke films, martial arts gore with people kicking each other to the other end of the planet and pornography. And they want one per night. So the ship's welfare fund no longer buys, but hires, 31 videos per round trip from some sleaze bag outfit in Belgium who are contracted to supply a selection of thrillers, sci-fi, action, comedies, and the perversely named adult. They are all dross and they have usually been copied from TV.

Tonight in the officers' lounge, it's *Barbarian at the Gate*, a true story of a company buyout of Nabisco the biscuit makers, featuring James Garner in a heavy corset and a terrible script, and Jonathan Pryce trying to make clichés live. This is almost worth watching as he sometimes pulls it off. The women are dumb and decorative and as real as Barbie, the humour is anal, and the power-dressed walk in and out of glassy skyscrapers. No cliché is too feeble to include. Naturally, all the complex finance is way above Garner's partner's head but she is able to coo and wind herself around him like a cat, which no doubt delays his heart attack. She does not, however, straighten his wandering toupee, which is shiny enough to reflect her sympathetic pout. We last an hour for, try as we might, we cannot concentrate. And we did try

THE CARIBBEAN

During the night, we pass through the Sombrero Passage into the Caribbean, and at 4.30am, I get my first glimpse of Saint John's in the Virgin Islands, where a large cruise ship is strung with lights like pearls and the whole scene is floodlit by the moon. When I wake for good at six, a whale is diving very near the bow, Saint Croix is to port and the huge silver moon is sitting on one horizon, with the rising sun on the other. Utterly wonderful.

On Puerto Rico radio they are playing Bach's *Christmas Oratorio*, a truly exciting work, and at breakfast we munch our Shredded Wheat and muesli to *Silent Night* and *O Come All Ye Faithful* on the dining room sound system. It's Christmas Eve and fiesta time.

'I suppose you wish you were with your family,' I say to Juan when he brings my toast and tea.

'Ma'am?' he's not sure what I mean and, when I repeat it without conviction, he says, 'I don't expect it Ma'am. It is a long time since I was there at Christmas.' I always forget that Filipinos don't go in for wishing they were elsewhere, not seriously anyway. And especially not on a day which includes major celebrating with parlour games and prizes.

At lunchtime, everyone knocks off, and about two the Filipinos mount a pig on a spit near the pool and we all stand about with cans of beer and take turns at winding. From time to time, someone dives into the pool, darts about like a fish and comes out shaking himself. The air is full of laughter and smoke as the taut little body becomes more shiny and golden, and drips more and more sacrificial fat into the tray. To show how easily I move between cultures (thanks to The Book), I give the spit a few festive turns, trying not to gag on the smell, weep in the smoke, or otherwise spoil the fun and the photos.

12 My turn to wind

'I don't remember sacrificial slaughter being mentioned in the marriage vows,' I say in case H thinks all this is second nature and not another marginally repellent episode in my trailing career. Naturally, he hopes I'm joking.

Our capers are briefly watched by a United States helicopter buzzing about, banking away and then coming back (understandably) for a second look. They're checking we're not discharging noxious substances, i.e. bilge that hasn't been through the oily water separator or worse. Our wake is a chortling blue white. Sludgy brownness or patches that look like puddles in a petrol station forecourt are bad signs. Huge fines, even prison for the master can result.

Eventually, everyone wanders off, leaving the pig to the galley staff, and I lie flat out on the loose covers listening to a performance of *Don Giovanni* from the Metropolitan Opera in New York which is booming in from nearby Puerto Rico. It almost obliterates the picture of the stuck pig, and I'm certainly enjoying all these sublime musical phrases.

At eight, we all assemble—well scrubbed—in the officers' lounge. The monster karaoke speakers and massive chilly bin they call the coffin, have been lugged up from the crew bar, the fairy lights on the Christmas tree are lit up and flashing, but only because they are shorting, and there is much shuffling, clearing of throats and smiling. As we wait for the ceremonies to begin, we all study our programmes, on the front of which is a naked baby lying in snow outside a church and inside lists the 22 items to come. Through the sliding doors in the dining room, I can see the pig—an apple in its mouth and holly poked into various parts of its body.

H's opening remarks are brief—he hopes we will all have a happy Christmas and enjoy the celebrations that the catering department have worked so hard to create. This brevity clearly disappoints, and while some look surprised, the cook looks as though he might cry. He clearly expected a great deal more, and stares at the space where H had stood long after he has sat down.

H makes a note for future fiestas—flagging-out is one long learning curve—and eventually the second officer rises portentously to say Grace. Feasting is item 2, and the second officer the highest-ranking Filipino. 'Bless us O Lord, and these thy gifts which of thy bounty we are about to receive, through Christ Our Lord'. 'Amen,' say the rest of us, and I am back at our red dining room table, hearing the deep weary timbre of my mother's voice saying those exact words as she untied her pinny and sat down to yet another meal. The Catholic Church really is universal; no matter where you go in the world children, the nuns assured us, you will always find the Latin mass and be at home (spiritually). Well they were wrong about that, but grace in the Caribbean is near enough. Imagine stumbling across the true meaning of catholic after all these years.

Close up, the table looks incredibly professional. Apart from the prostrate pig, it is splashed with colour—poinsettias, exotic fruits, and greenery—and piled with chicken, prawns, cold meat, spring rolls, salads, paella and every fresh tropical fruit going. There's even neat little bowls of crème caramel. It's the work of Romeo—a talented able seaman—who has served his time on the *QE2* and clearly learnt what to do with pigs, apples and poinsettias to please the palates of the high payers.

13 The captain starts the feast

When the pig has been reduced to a skeleton and the table looks as though a gale has blown across it, we reassemble in the lounge to listen to the chief cook, our preacher for the evening. With his face on solemn, a wad of notes to hand and his throat well cleared, he asks us to imagine we are sitting on a hillside near Bethlehem, watching a family arriving to pay their taxes: a man, a woman and a donkey. 'Imagine,' he says casting his eyes from one to the other like a real pro, 'how they feel after their long journey. The woman is with child, and the man is anxious to find a place where she can lay her head.' She'll be feeling utterly ghastly, I imagine. Her legs will be bloated, and her head throbbing. She'll have never felt worse, in fact. Imagine your waters about to break and spending your day on a donkey. She's possibly been sick, her lower back will be killing her and perhaps permanently damaged, the ass's bones will be digging in, and varicose veins will be making her legs like Stilton.

'The woman's name is Mary and her husband is Joseph, and they have come far. Very Far.'

And she'll be cursing the Roman git with white hands and wall-to-wall servants, whose idea this was. Just when she needed to be at home, she has been sent this hell. She may be saying, 'Joseph, you may not be the father, but if you don't find somewhere soon, we're going to lose this child and you know what that means to the world.' Oh Mary, don't exaggerate.

'Just as they are turned away from the last place, the star stops. It stops above a stable, not far from the inn.' With this being only item 4 of the 22 and there being no sign of labour, I am visualising being there forever. But just before my back collapses in sympathy and I visualise going on the rampage on Mary's behalf, he gathers up his notes and it is time, at last, for the 'Parlour games with Prizes' and I am up on the floor judging the beer-drinking competition which follows the statue-dancing contest, and then we are all throwing darts in blindfolds.

14 Throwing darts in blindfolds

Between each nail biting event, the music is turned up to raucous and the third engineer, doing an excellent Michael Jackson, writhes and screams at us all to join in. His eyes blaze and every part of his spare frame moves independently at such speed he is almost a blur. The chief dances manfully too, but H and the mate refuse and I feel that judging competitions while passive smoking is as far as I'm prepared to go. Raising my heart-lung capacity in this atmosphere could hasten my end and no one is going to thank me afterwards.

15 Eating an apple on a string

I'm already coughing in painful spasms and every time I am about to congratulate myself on having finished a can of some unspeakable, very cold softie without burping or throwing up, another one is put in front of me and I wish they were not so attentive and polite. They, as ever, are all drinking Bacardi by the tumbler and not falling over or being loutish, which is one of those cultural differences I have never fathomed. Particularly as they are all slighter than many a British female and we are always told that body mass is the key to how much one can drink.

After each wild dance, the third engineer collapses dramatically between the oiler and the messman, his eyes bulging and his spent arms draped about their necks. For some reason Filipinos like to sit on top of one another. There may be 24 seats for 24, and while we will claim at least two each, they will squash together onto as few as possible. This could be quite good in the lifeboat.

In item 12—Group Spooning of Peanuts—there is a hint of trouble. The idea is to get a pile of nuts from one saucer to another using only a teaspoon in the mouth. It's tricky, it's hilarious (preferably if you are prepuberty) and the engine department lose because, screeches the third engineer, jumping up and down, the bosun ate his. 'He did, Sir. He did.' And we all fall about broken by the naked wit of the bosun and the fact that nobody really minds a spot of cheating. It's all part of the high spirits. But the third engineer is also saying he never moved in the statue dancing (Item 5) but was pushed by the wiper, which calls my judging into question, which is so unthinkable we laugh ourselves ragged.

Fortunately, the slight hint that his outrage may be real soon disappears. An able seaman cranks up the karaoke and dedicates his crooning of *On Top of Old Smoky* to the third engineer and harmony is restored, especially when the third engineer wins first prize by miles for eating an apple suspended on a string with his hands tied behind his back. This is impossible, and most fall defeated to the floor while the third engineer kneels before the swinging apple, contorts his head and jabs at it maniacally until his bared teeth penetrate just enough for purchase. Soon his entire jaw is wrapped about the shining skin and he is taking bite after bite as though he is devouring a prey. He stops only when there is nothing at all left, not even a pip. 'He's on something,' I say to the chief when the third engineer is writhing in triumph, eyes bulging, veins throbbing in his temples, and sweat coursing in runnels from his forehead. 'He's always full-on at parties,' the chief says, and the mate agrees, 'It's normal for him to look as though he's stuffed himself with uppers and to swing between hyperactive and normal, with brief intervals of coma. He's a good engineer, though. He gives everything big licks.'

'Looks clinical to me,' I say, and H smiles uncertainly, knowing my track record for spotting the haywire.

Item 22, the last, is Giving of Gifts—Captain and Wife. With the atmosphere back to sober, H calls each name, shakes each hand and I present them with a box of Belgian chocolates, courtesy of the charterer. Despite the rattle in my smoke-filled lungs, I smile and wish them a happy Christmas on behalf of the owner, the charterer, and the various management companies and, minutes before I become totally loco myself, I rush out on deck to gulp lungfuls of Caribbean air, and to reassure myself that I haven't just imagined the whole thing.

Not long after we went to bed, the third engineer attacked the wiper, first with the karaoke microphone, and then a Bacardi bottle. Fortunately, the mate grabbed his arm seconds before the bottle sliced through the wiper's head. The consequences, had he succeeded, do not bear thinking about, so, after breakfast, the third engineer is in the Merchant Navy equivalent of a court, presided over by H, the chief and the mate. It goes something like this:

'Did you intend to hit this man?'

'Yes, Sir.'

'Did you mean to hurt this man?'

'Yes, Sir.'

'Why did you do it?'

'He was laughing at me, and I told him to stop, and he didn't.'

'Why was he laughing at you?'

'I don't know, Sir. He thought I was joking.'

'About what?'

'About the party, Sir. Some of the Filipinos were starting to leave and many people had gone to a lot of trouble to give them a good party, and they didn't appreciate this and I was annoyed, Sir. I wanted everyone to enjoy the party.'

'Were you going to hit him with the Bacardi bottle?'

'Yes, Sir.'

The third engineer is logged—i.e. it is recorded in the log book with all the official ship's business and for all who matter to see—and told that at the slightest sign of trouble he'll be off. He has done irreparable damage to the atmosphere among the Filipinos, but clearly feels he has right on his side.

It's a bad start to a stunningly beautiful day. A few delicate, golden-white clouds, like meringues, are dotted here and there in the deepest blue, and we are rocking gently towards our ETA at Moín in Costa Rica, our first port.

To me, as a reluctant caterer, Christmas at sea is a miracle. Not that I ever get used to regularly appearing food at any time of the year. But on the big occasions, having staff certainly makes celebrating easy, as the hardest thing I have to do is find some tropical chic to float about in, sip gin and tonics, and scatter pleasantries and *bon mots* without giving a thought to whether the sprouts are going mushy, or the brandy sauce is sticking to the pan, which it certainly would be if I were responsible.

So while the Filipinos fill the afterdeck with the sizzle and smell of barbecued this and fried rice that, we sit sedately in the cool hush of the saloon, pulling crackers and tucking into turkey, stuffing and pudding with brandy sauce. Afterwards we relax in the lounge with coffee and liqueurs, as though the days of grocers (as chief stewards were known) were not long gone, and we were not about to follow them.

After the feasting, the ship is like a tomb with only the watch keepers stirring. But when it starts to get dark, everyone gradually emerges from sleep or the video room and when we wander down to the evening barbecue the third officer is holding forth about pirates, one of his favourite topics. 'Have you been boarded, Ma'am?' he asks, beaming. It is an idyll of a Caribbean evening: just the right temperature with no wind, stars beginning to prick the darkening sky and only the gentlest movement. When I shake my head, he says, 'I was on a ship that was always between the Melaka and Singapore Straits and Indonesia and nowhere else, and we were boarded six times. Six times!' He whistles. 'It was awful. And no one helped us. When we asked for help from the Singapore Navy they did nothing. But,' he waggles his finger in the air, 'they were always in the area.'

The third officer considers this incontrovertible evidence that the Singapore Navy were responsible. Not that they did the dirty work—that was done by Indonesians—but they were the profiteers. This is not a new theory. Well-organised piracy is big business, and those creaming off the greatest profit are far from the sea and danger, probably living safely in Hong Kong, Singapore, Taiwan, China or even London. Some piracy may be small and opportunistic, but the big hauls are well planned and they know all about you, and exactly what you are carrying.

'These pirates knew we had money and were only doing 12 knots, so we didn't have a chance. Six times we were boarded, Ma'am. But they didn't have guns, just long knives with poison on the tips.' This is not what I want to hear, but the third officer thinks I am gripped. 'We got so fed up in the end, because we didn't have anything except the hoses which didn't scare anyone, so I told the fitter to make up arrows, large arrows,' (he indicates something spear sized), 'and we waited for the next alarm, and we were going to kill them all, Ma'am, and throw their bodies into the water.' Seeing me blanch, he smiles, 'really Ma'am, these are not good people and they do not deserve to live.' I don't argue. It's Christmas, and the third officer knows what good people are and who deserves to live, and the fact that they were mere employees doesn't count, and certainly isn't grounds in his book for sparing them the fitter's spear.

Fortunately (for the pirates and the third officer who may otherwise now be incarcerated), the alarm was not raised, and the pirates came and went unmolested once more.

COSTA RICA: MOÍN AND LIMÓN

H is up at 2am, and all I remember is, 'don't forget to lock up if you get up to see the arrival.' At 6am, I wake again to an exquisite morning with Costa Rica slowly rising from the sea, the great Cerro Matama drawing grey and purple lines which rise and dip like an ever-expanding graph above the golden horizon. Then the vegetation-covered foreground hills appear and swoop and dive about the coast like huge birds.

To port lies Limón and its offshore island, Isla Uvita; Moín and the much smaller Isla de Pájaros are to starboard. Columbus saw all this. On his fourth and last visit in 1502, he landed on Isla Uvita and was made so welcome by the gold-wearing indigenas, that he wrongly assumed that some wealthy, well-organised society waited for Spain in the hinterland, and that El Costa Rica, as he called it, would be well worth grabbing.

But he was wrong; all attempts to settle the coast failed and the Spanish trekked in and up to their highland cities leaving the Province of Limón, which stretches from Nicaragua to Panama, to the lush unconquerable richness of its flora and fauna and later to the labour brought in to work the plantations. As a result today the province is 18% of the country but has only 7% of the population. But Limón is Costa Rica's principal port and every kind of ship—bulk carrier, container, ro-ro, tankers and cruise ships—steam in and out, and a reasonably-sized town now sprawls around it.

At Moín, where we are heading, there is nothing at all, except the odd bar and dwelling and a constant procession of banana trucks. The docks were developed in 1982, in anticipation of the boom in the banana trade following the dismantling of tariff barriers, and the great new age of free trade which was to follow. It hasn't yet happened because of the long running and complex Banana Wars which began in the early 1990s, when the United States reported the European Union to the World Trade Organisation accusing them of flouting global rules by favouring bananas from former British and French colonies.

All around the coast, great white fountains constantly erupt as the ocean hurls itself against huge reddy-brown boulders, strewn about like giant gobstoppers. The golden blue sky is cloudless, except for a few trails of lint, and some plumper wads of luminous white sitting on the peaks like jaunty sun hats. Beyond Bahía de Moín, where the straight coast stretches south towards Panama, there are patches where sand glints, but mostly the green lushness tumbles to the water's edge. Here and there, a single tin roof or a window flashes as it catches the light, and on the headland above the roaring surf sit a collection of what look like large straw hats, but are in fact thatched hotel chalets. Myriad greens cover the coast with only the occasional burst of bright orange or deep red.

Near Isla de Pájaros a very tall, craggy Dutch pilot, resembling a gnarled tree with two wavy branches, climbs the ladder and a short time later we are tied up between a rusty Dole refrigerated ship (a reefer) and a pristine white Del Monte one and the crew are getting the cranes going and opening the hatches. The water is as still as laminate and the air thick with butterflies the size of small wrens splashing white, yellow, black and sapphire everywhere. There are birds too, chirrupy swift-like darters skimming the water, and crows strutting or poking about and rearranging rubbish on the docks.

Close up, Puerto Moín is not a beautiful place. The dock itself is a great swathe of concrete, with one long open-sided shed with a tin roof and, across the water, heaps of gravel and rusty hulks are piled up where the River Moín is being diverted in preparation for more berths, but no work is in progress.

Costa Rica is one of the original banana republics, and trading in what are now called 'dollar' bananas (the US may not produce them, but owns the means of production) has been going on here since the last quarter of the 19th century. Following the development of refrigerated sea transport and the building of the Central American railway, the United Fruit Company—now Chiquita but then called Mama Yunai (Momma United)—took over the 'care' of Costa Rica, Panama, Honduras and Guatemala, governing them in all but name. In 1923, Standard Fruit and Steamship Company (Dole) began trading, and later Del Monte, and today these three multinationals still own thousands of hectares in Latin America, and despite competition from British, Colombian and Ecuadorean companies, their 'dollar' bananas account for more than 70% of world trade, with Moín being one of their most important outlets.

The agent's assistant, Ben, gives me a lift to Limón. A descendant of the Jamaicans they brought in to build the railways, his spare, rangy body moves fluently in his khaki trousers.

The road isn't busy, but it is so badly potholed that he thinks nothing of mounting the pavement on the wrong side or careering down the middle of the road only to swerve or brake violently just before we hit something. I suppress screeches and the desire to throttle him and push my heart out of my throat with deep breathing and I try to concentrate on the rampant vegetation which is broken only occasionally by a cluster of houses at the roadside or set snootily back, all of which are covered in luridly painted grills often in liturgical purple. 'The government has promised to fix all this,' says Ben with a deep, musical laugh. 'Fat chance, man. Promises,' meaning that Limón is the last place they'll get good roads; the highlanders don't have to use them.

In Limón, he drops me in the square where tourists are standing around buses about to go to more interesting places, or mooching about on the beach opposite where rollers are breaking over smooth and shiny laval rock. A few tourists are wandering towards the town. Just beyond the square, two gleaming white cruise ships tower over the dock where a line of sanitised market stalls are being set up.

16 Park Vargas, Limón

17 Limón street

In the middle of the square, the Park Vargas is full of regimented rows of very tall palm trees whose lower trunks are painted white against marauding ants. Birds are squawking all around, but I catch only the occasional streak of yellow or a long black tail. Turning in circles, my upturned eyes narrowed against the light, I search for Limón's number one tourist attraction, the three-toed sloths. Seeing me, a small wizened man smiles and crooks his finger and I follow him past dilapidated statuary, bits of stone seats lying where they have fallen in the 1991 earthquake, and a 'seen-better-days' band rotunda. He points a wizened finger to what looks like a speeded up film of a branch growing or a large bat doing Tai Chi and smiles toothlessly. 'Like you?' he says and then he glowers horribly at a small group of Japanese men who have appeared from nowhere and followed us.

'Love them,' I say, 'always have.' I gush to make up for my lack of Spanish and he cackles appreciatively, the lines on his face creasing until his eyes almost disappear. When he shuffles off chuckling and I flop onto a crumbling bench, I can suddenly see them everywhere, mostly in cosy clusters pretending to be growths where the branches fork, but some loners are creeping almost imperceptibly along a branch towards a new feast of leaves, their main diet. Apparently, they can take several days digesting food and when they excrete they make the enormous journey to the ground, possibly to feed the tree where they live. Astonishing that this laudable, economic industry gave its name to one of the seven deadly sins. Well, maybe not.

Sloths are just one face of Costa Rica's enormously diverse flora and fauna. Here, they sell eco-tourism, and 12% of the country—which is only two-thirds the size of Scotland—is National Parks. But despite having the most enlightened ecology programmes in Latin America, and a stable democracy, the forest is disappearing. Until recently, cattle ranching, now in decline, was responsible. Now, deforestation happens in the name of bananas. 'Slicing the rainforest onto your cornflakes' is one way it is described. Dollar banana plantations don't just cut down trees; they destroy the land beyond reclaiming. Then they take more. Already 80,000 hectares in Costa Rica have had to be abandoned and more land claimed either from small farmers or from the forest. The average plantation gives 30 years before the land is so depleted it is unfit for anything.

A short, dapper man wearing a vat of hair cream and trotting purposefully suddenly stops in front of me. 'And where might you be from?' he says importantly and I tell him politely, but without smiling in case he really is a nosy git as opposed to a friendly Tico. 'I have made a tour of Scotland, England and Earland,' he says with lashings of pomp, 'Welcome to Costa Rica,' and he bows slightly and leaves. I watch as his small steps cross the road between the tourist buses and disappear behind the huge dark wooden doors of the Palacio Municipal.

Ticos, as Costa Ricans call themselves, are known for their friendliness. It is their hallmark, or so every page of the tourist literature says. They are also the happiest and most fun-loving people on the earth. There are none happier, none more deliriously jocose. (Except perhaps the West Australians, whose guidebooks make similar claims.) But in general, I am not overwhelmed with *bonhomie*. In the shops, there is a sort of studied indifference and the odd time I do want to enquire about something I almost have to make a citizen's arrest. In the Municipal Market, a series of dark, crumbling, smelly alleys, the shops and stalls are cramped and full of cheap plastic goods. Every general store is full of artificial flowers and withered Christmas trees draped with files of tinsel, and the supermarket is a long squat heap of concrete that looks like a prison and—like many supermarkets—has the aesthetic appeal of a rat's nest.

Inside, I meet a wall of personality-distorting music and immediately forget who I am and why I am there, so order a coffee from one of the fast-food stalls in the reverberative communal eating space, mouthing my order to someone in a pink hairnet, a pink polycotton overall and a pink peaked cap who looks like a marching girl. She punches one of a bank of computers and asks me if I want egg with it, which alerts me to the fact that I have just paid far too many colónes for a coffee and am in line for a hamburger.

Naturally, there is nothing she can do as she points at the A4 printout for one hamburger without egg, and then at the computer, and then at the person in a hairnet behind a counter at the back, where flotillas of pink hairnets are screaming orders at one another, and says I can have coffee to the value of and she'll forget the hamburger.

I shrug hopelessly, and she shrugs and I shrug again until we have bonded as victims of technology (and noise) and I sit at one of the pink plastic bolted-down tables and chairs and wait for the vat of coffee that will take me all day to drink and possibly speed up my heartbeat fatally. All around me, people are holding onto their hair and polystyrene containers because, above our heads and adding to the pandemonium, giant fans are generating localised whirlwinds. I am struck by the huge variety of genetic types, none of them particularly Hispanic and many of them—especially the women—not awfully robust-looking, apart that is from the strong-boned, tall Jamaican descendants. 'They don't like the Jamaicans,' the Dutch pilot had said, 'It's not that they're Jamaicans; it's the way they live.' 'They' are the highlanders, the descendants of the Spanish who founded the cities where the majority live today, viz. Cartago, Heredia, San José—the capital—and Alajuela.

Many who now live in and around Limón can trace their descendants either to slavery or to the labour brought in for the railways and the coffee and banana plantations in the late 1800s. In Costa Rica, Jamaicans are 2% of the population; in Limón they are nearer 33%.

Just as I am about to leave, the pink hairnet reappears. Her tiny hands are full of colónes and her thin mouth and sharp, enormous eyes are beaming. She has persuaded the computer to give me a refund. Ticas really are friendly, I think, as she backs away, shyly apologising.

Outside, the streets are full of honking taxis offering me tours, smelly drains and women in precipitous heels teetering about in packs. Sometimes they congregate near dark bars pulsing with wailing music in which I can see people writhing like maggots in a blackout. The men take long strides, as though they are eating the pavement with their legs and click their fingers or press flesh in the air when they meet.

Back at the cruise berths, the Limón experience is up and running. In the international phoning tent, jolly queues in easy-care casuals from the *Vistafjord* and *Regent Star* are comparing Panama Canal transits and destinations, and it is all so sanitised that the smelly drains and litter, and the emaciated and destitute of Limón, just up the road, seem to be another planet. Some do go as far as the sloths and the tourist buses, but it's mainly the eager young Scandinavians and Filipino crews who go further.

Trade is brisk. The leather bags, lacework and wooden boxes are all being admired and the coffee is shifting fast, although everyone— provedores and agents anyway—always say the best beans go to the United States, and you can buy better and fresher wherever you live. But that's not true of the large fabric parrots which are today's must-have, the larger and more disagreeable looking the better. Everyone walking up both gangways has a parrot in one hand and a forest of tropical flowers in the other. At least the flowers will die which is what all decent souvenirs you can't eat should do, and preferably long before you have to lug them home. As travel trash, fabric parrots are on a par with huge Mexican hats; there is simply nothing you can do with them once you get them home. But at least they will never suddenly screech as you pass them in your living room, as though you are personally responsible for their virulent plumage and grumpy disposition.

Through the large windows of the *Vistafjord*—a luxury Cunard liner—parrots are propped up at morning coffee or bridge, while others are flat out beside recliners where their new owners are reading or snoozing. How their friends must dread these presents, I'm thinking, when a particularly dyspeptic parrot clips me round the ear. 'I'm sorry,' I hear myself say to a man with bushy nostril hair. He moves closer and looks suspiciously into my face as though he is wondering whether I have a gun. Then he says slowly and slightly menacingly, 'How do you do? I'm Jed and this here's Beth. We're on the *Vista Feeord* and it's wonderful.'

'Really?' I squeak with mock jauntiness, 'very nice to meet you.' He relaxes, but is still close enough for me to see that his mad blue eyes are flecked with what looks like traces of pus, which may mean a dicky liver.

'It's wonderful,' he says again, assuming I'm from the less classy *Regent Star*, 'but you pay. You sure as hell pay. But the service—you can't fault the service. Tell her, honey. Tell her.' Honey doesn't want to, and doesn't see why she should. 'You know. Tell her about the service. You know better than I do,' he whines, threatening to sulk.

She glowers and I can see she is thinking he's pulled this stunt once too often, and I am hoping that I'm not the spark that will light the fuse that is going to blow up their marriage. and me with it. But no. She starts, very quietly at first, but we both breathe out and I beam encouragement. 'I've cruised for years. This is my third since last summer, and to tell you the truth, I have to say this is the best. *The best.'* I beam more. He moves his cheeks out a bit and I think he thinks he's smiling. 'But you pay,' he says quietly so as not to stop her flow. 'You sure as hell pay. Give her an example, honey.'

'Well, say on any other ship, if I said to the staff, say, 'can you tell me where I might get a teaspoon?', they'd invariably say, 'over there, in the third drawer down,' or wherever. Well, on *Queuenard* you say you wanna teaspoon and they drop what they're doing and say, "come with me," and they take you there and put it in your hand and take you back,' which strikes me as odd. If you sure as hell pay, why the hell don't they fetch it, but I say nothing.

'But of course you pay. You sure as hell pay,' he says again, meaning it hurts just a bit. 'But you can't fault the staff,' he says. 'They are wonderful. Won-der-ful. But as I said, it's all on the bill, and they expect you to notice what isn't. Know what I mean?' I do. I sure as hell do. 'I'm retired now, and I bet you'd like to hear about all the things I've done since I packed it in last summer.' Of course I would; it goes without saying. So he says, 'I would have packed it in earlier but Beth here,' he nods in her direction, 'Beth said no, because she needed the money to cruise.'

For this, Beth wants to throttle him with the parrot, but instead she mutters something pianissimo, along the lines of, 'honey you're dreaming,' which he doesn't hear. Deafness is such a marriage saver, or can be. 'Since last summer, when I finally packed it in, you won't believe this'—I will, I know a cruise junkie when I get near one—'I've been on three cruises and been home only long enough to hold a huge barbie for my son's clients, 200 of them, and I had to start from scratch building the damned barbie he needed one so goddam big. Anyway, no sooner was that done than we were off again to India, Sri Lanka, Thailand, Malaysia, Singapore, and some goddam place I'd never heard of and have forgotten again and here's me taught school all my life, history and geography. Never mind,' he goes on. 'You won't believe this, but the travel agent phoned when we got home and said they had this 109 day cruise and were we interested and we said we'll phone back, and when we phoned and said no they said well how about this *Queuenard* one, and ... well ... here we are.' We all smile and nod and he says, 'What about yourself? How's things on the *Regent Star?*' And when I tell him I'm on a banana boat in Moín, he whistles through his teeth and says, 'Well how about that,' a couple of times, and 'that must be interesting, don't you think, honey?' while I smile feebly, thinking it would be interesting with stabilisers and he says, 'You know what? We've been to I don't know how many countries since we retired, but we've never been on a freighter. Never. But we take the magazine, you know this little magazine they have in the States and, you never know, one day we might just do it. What do you think, honey?'

To be practical, I mention the making your own entertainment, the short time in port, the lack of laid-on tours and the morning sickness. 'Oh yeah, oh yeah,' he waves all this away impatiently just as I am warming to the deterrents knowing that the sight of him coming up the gangway would do me no good at all. 'We don't mind all that, do we honey?' Honey's nodding; every time she starts a sentence, she's too late. ''Cos you know what, I wanna write a book real bad. And I figure a freighter might be just the place.'

'Really?' I squeak.

'I wanna write a book an yi know what I wanna write a book about?' I don't, and I don't like the way he's stepped forward again and is thinking of grabbing my non-existent lapels. 'Well lemme tell you.' His voice has gone uninflected, he's eliding all over the place and all the syllables have dashes between them. 'I-wan-na- wrid-a-book,' ('Sing it,' I feel like saying) and suddenly he speeds up, 'about all the bastards I've known. All those wall-eyed clowns who've done me down. Yeah. That's what I wanna write a book about,' and he steps back, his eyes narrowed so I can't see the pussy bits and his head nodding in a deranged way.

'Good luck,' I say chirpily. 'A freighter might be just the ticket,' I add putting my arm out stiffly and shaking both their hands. 'Enjoy the rest of your cruise.'

'Cripes,' I think, as I stagger away. 'There are people paying Cunard prices to meet that!' And you sure as hell pay.

Mention Limón in nautical circles and chances are someone will start talking about the America Bar and what a great night they had there. How legless they got, how many women they you-know-what-I-meaned, and then they will say, 'Of course, it's all boarded up now.' The America bar is to Limón what the 60s are to last century: all other bars and decades pale.

I find the boarded-up shell of the legendary bar, and next door, perhaps risen from its ashes, is the Restaurant Brisas del Caribe, which is clean, light and airy, with a tiled floor, lots of fans, and gentle background music. I sit for a while, drinking ginger ale, watching the crowds go by and wondering why anyone would want to cruise Cunard and be taken by the hand to get a teaspoon and spend every night eating with someone who was thinking about all those wall-eyed clowns who'd done him down. (Why wall-eyed?)

Every few minutes, someone comes in selling lottery tickets (the universal symbol of hope that has taken over from lighting candles in church), jewellery or flowers, and the affluent-looking local customers wave them away without interrupting their conversations on their mobiles, or with their well-turned-out companions. It's an upmarket place and it has what I desperately hope is a toilet to match. But no; behind the pretty door, it stinks and there is no water. Still, I've seen as bad in many a place, including the United Kingdom. Deeply unpleasant toilets are part of life, wherever. As is holding your nose, shutting your eyes and using them.

Oscar, my taxi driver, is another beautiful Afro-Rican with a mop of shiny curls and excellent English. Business is good. 'Oh yeah, man. I'm busy. Two cruise ships is unusual, but they can guarantee one every week. Wednesdays, usually.'

'The same day as us.'

'Yeah?' He looks at me through the rear vision mirror with new interest. 'You're in for the whole day? You'd like a tour?' I nod. 'No problem. I can do you two hours to San José—it normally takes two and a half—I'll show you the city, and on the way back we can see the rainforest, then a plantation so you can see our great bananas, then the exotic birds and a flower garden.' I study the tariff waving about from the dash. Catching me, he says, 'Oh, that's for cruisers; working ships get a special rate.' Of course, cruisers are there to be ripped off. He laughs, knowing what I'm thinking. 'Next time you're in, call and ask for Oscar.'

It is tempting, but H has been on a hair-raising two hours on the wrong side of the road overtaking on blind bends trip to San José, and I know he won't be keen. And what if we break down and they leave without me? And they do. Greens they wait for; partners and non-essential crew they leave. All the same, I take his card and ask him to pull into the Hotel Maribu Caribe so I can check it out just in case H can manage to get away for dinner.

After the noise and dilapidation of Limón, the hotel's lush and manicured beauty wrapped in a reverential hush, disturbed only by the pounding of distant surf, is difficult to take in. But this is eco-tourist habitat, and if not exactly how the locals live, certainly how they know we like to live. This is a common trailing experience. In many places, I have my nose rubbed in the glaring inequities my comforts are predicated on and, of course, I cannot do anything more than smile feebly at unfortunates and try to maximise my awareness of just how the planet is plundered on my behalf and attempt to minimise it. It's a hopeless ambition and possibly futile, but it doesn't stop me trying to clean up my own act and, when possible, avoid the treadmill of galloping consumption and discarding which a constantly expanding economy demands of us all. I am also aware that contributing to the local economy is usually a positive.

The hotel is very seductive. The rooms, the circular thatched chalets I mistook for sunhats from the sea, are dotted about the open-air café and pool, rather like a tribal village, and the restaurant is perched on the cliff, its semi-circular dining balcony giving stunning glimpses, through gaps in glossy vegetation, of the sea battering the cliffs below. Over the tops of the trees, I can see an expanse of calm blue sea sparkling away to the horizon, with the banana boats trickling in and out of Moín looking like very cute toys.

The restaurant is empty. The *maître d'* is flat out and apparently asleep on top of a waiter, but they both leap up when I cough, quickly straighten themselves and one dives for menus and water while the other pushes me into a seat. Business is not brisk, Oscar told me, and I could get good discounts because of what he called 'these ridiculous reports in the US press about Costa Rica being dangerous'. He was annoyed because his business is suffering. 'One American is murdered and they're all screaming and saying criminals are targeting tourists. Truth is, man, they're far more likely to be robbed at home.'

Beside the pool, two bodies wearing a few bits of string are flat out on recliners like discarded Barbies and Kens. As I sit with my coffee, she gets up as languorously as a cat (unlike Barbie who is a stranger to sensuality), and sways to the bar where she settles her G-string, arranges her disciplined buttocks on a high stool, and orders a drink in German. Astonishingly, she seems totally covered by her token clothing; she certainly does not feel exposed. Nor is she reduced to flesh, beautiful though it is. Back at the pool, he stands, stretches, and shimmies into the water very un-Kenishly.

Near me, a giant white man in preppy chinos and even preppier glasses, whose extra-long legs are under his large chin, briefly stops painstakingly covering a huge pile of postcards with minute writing, to watch first her and then him. His eyes narrow judgementally.

Suddenly, a shower of laughter makes us all turn, and a party of sun hats and silk swish by, fanning themselves. Uniformed lackeys follow, carrying matching luggage. When they disappear into the vegetation, the hush is broken only by Ken impersonating a dolphin, distant voices from reception and the occasional clink of ice. We are surrounded by rows of neat identical flowering shrubs, thick-bladed mown grass, and well-cared-for stone paths. Beyond the chalets, the hyperactive jungle is one season from taking over.

It is as unreal as a film and as good a mock-up of paradise as I've seen. Gazing at the spectacular oceanic view, I think not just about dinner, but perhaps about moving in until H's tour of duty is over. Unfortunately, just as I get to reception to ask about the tariff and am wondering where the staff are, those same Japanese tourists appear and demand their valuables from the hotel safe. They rest their arms on the polished wood and stare through me as though I am a pot plant or virtually realised. Mysteriously, a bevy of receptionists also appears, but immediately disappears, jangling keys. Naturally, I am overcome by the need to kick them all out of the way, not to hurt them, but to see how they would react to assault by a strong invisible leg.

This is not my first brush with the male touring group. I remember vividly the time a similar one tried to suffocate me on the Sentosa Monorail in Singapore, when they all piled into my very small carriage as though it were empty. Invisibility would be pleasant if it were not life threatening, I thought, as they folded their arms, spread their knees wide and swivelled their heads in some arcane touring ritual. The themed Sentosa tat was so gripping they failed to hear my gasps or see my concertinaed form in the corner, which was incapable of defence or revenge—let alone speech. I was not then, and am not now, anti-Japanese. Colonising male behaviour can crop up anywhere. It is not nationality specific.

Back with Oscar in Moín, there is a huge queue of banana trucks at the dock gate and someone says there's a strike. 'That's normal,' says Oscar, 'It'll pass like a shower. It comes ten times a day. They stop, they shout, they sit, but they soon start again. No worries, man.' So I sit there not worrying, thinking how much I like this Aussie phrase and how it could transform my life. 'No worries, man' I'll say next time the company gives H two days' notice of leaving or worse, cancels his return flight and tells me he is not coming for another six weeks and calls it a hitch. 'No worries, man,' I'll say to personnel. Even under the most extreme provocation, 'no worries, man' must be more evolved than alternately weeping, and battering soft furnishings.

In shipping, nothing is certain. Never pack too early; your relief may never come. It's not all over until you see the whites of his eyes, they all say. And as for minibreaking, birthdays, weddings, and dental appointments, forget it. The only occasion a seaman is sure to make is his own funeral—or so they all add.

Near the ship, the noise is hellish. Banana boxes are jumping along on rattling conveyor belts and disappearing through holes in the ship's side I had no idea were there. I briefly wonder whether they could leak and/or stove in in heavy weather, or what would happen if someone forgot to shut them? Between the holes and the shed, yellow canopies are lolling on makeshift poles. The Caribbean coast, unlike the Pacific, has no dry season, and although some months are less wet, December isn't one of them.

There are men everywhere. From a line of large modern trucks, huge and athletic brown bodies shining with sweat are hauling the boxes out and slotting them into gaps on the fast moving crowded belt. This is heavy work, but they make it look easy. They could be playing basketball, or even dancing, as they bounce about in trainers, baseball caps, shorts and loose singlets.

18 Loading, Moín

As the boxes career noisily up and down their ball bearing hills, men on the ground make sure they don't derail or pile up. From time to time, they whip one off and pass it to a little island of makeshift tables where white, puffy men with clipboards and chubby hands open the airtight plastic and remove every last hand, as bunches are called. This is quality control; they are checking for yellows, substandards or infestations.

Every square inch of the dock is covered: men are slumped against pillars like stuffed toys, or stretched out asleep on idle bits of conveyor; men are selling ice-creams and cold drinks from hand-wheeled carts; groups of men are talking or playing cards; overseers are walking about bawling orders, or slapping people on the back, or gesticulating wildly. Before tomorrow, they have 110,000 boxes to load, all the bananas having been picked two days ago. It's a tight schedule for H, for the growers and for the shippers, and this rather disordered scene gives a lie to the multinational clout behind it.

At the top of the gangway, there is an overpowering stink of sludge, the waste product of the thousands of tonnes of fuel we have already used. In some places, they pay to take it away, in others they take it for nothing. Here, where it's spread on the dusty roads in banana plantations, the trucks charge $40 a tonne.

There is no sign of H, and then he waves from up forward where he's checking on the painting gang hired to paint the bow. Three of them are asleep and the foreman is rushing about gesticulating like a dysfunctional windmill, assuring H that the job's going well. The three bodies move slightly as I step over them. They look extremely comfortable, even graceful, on the hard, green, sun-drenched deck.

H tells me the agent has organised a plantation trip, but with only a few hours' sleep, the wiper who was hit with the mic to get to the doctor, plus surveyors, provedores, and fumigators to see, there's no chance of his going with me. We're both disappointed. Seeing a plantation is important, not only because bananas are paying the mortgage this trip, but also because we eat them and I like to know all about what I eat. All sorts of stuff can go on in my name if I have been drugged by the Musak of the supermarkets and the marketing messages of the multinationals and ask no questions about why it looks so perfect, and who or what died that I might eat.

Not long after lunch, as I am watching men deep in the hatches stowing banana boxes, smoke suddenly billows out of the fo'c'sle. In minutes the sea and sky have gone, a rough white blanket is all over the forward deck and I can just make out the mate staggering out of a hatch, coughing, looking extremely worried and starting to run. Ahead, a man is strolling toward the accommodation with what looks like a large bassoon. The mate stops, rubs his eyes and smiles sheepishly.

The fumigator—we had both forgotten. A few days ago a telex advised that all ships going to Colombia that have been in any other Caribbean port, had to be sprayed to destroy the mosquito which causes dengue (pronounced dhen gay) fever, a virus spread by the Aedes mosquito who bite by day and live in standing water in urban tropical areas. Because you can be as vulnerable inside as out, the accommodation has to be done and a few minutes later the radio officer and several other men are at my door, white clouds swirling about behind them. 'It's not dangerous,' says Sparkie smiling, 'you don't need to go,' he adds sweetly. I am appalled at his misplaced faith, but I say nothing and rush down the stairs in a fog that is trying to claw out my larynx and lungs.

PLANTATION VISIT

On the way to the plantation, the driver stops in Limón at the agent's office to collect Ben, my guide and minder. We head south along the coast, over the Cieneguita river past a Seventh Day Adventist Church (I make a note to tell Sparkie), and houses which look cobbled together from corrugated iron, breeze block, or wood which the sun has bleached of all colour. No two are alike, even vaguely, and while most are basic and undecorated, the more elaborate are covered in bright blue or purple grills. Occasionally there is a burst of bougainvillea or a lolling lilac bush as well as quite a few hibiscus hedges, while all along the dusty road people walk purposefully or amble in hip-swaying groups, while around and among them cyclists weave careful paths.

Away to our left in Limón Bay, four ships are at anchor and one of the great white fleet, as Chiquita's ships are known, is alongside. 'Moín is congested,' Ben says, 'some are loading in Limón.' A small plane circling the anchorage comes down beside the driftwood-scattered beach and taxis towards a toy town terminal, where there is a windsock and a few parked cars but not much else. 'Limón's airport. There are three planes a day to San José if you want to go next time.' I smile and say 'maybe,' already knowing that if I'm going to risk being left behind it will be for a national park or a beach full of turtles at least.

The road south to Panama is good; there are no potholes, not much traffic and, to begin with, it runs beside the sea on the low-lying Caribbean coast. Away from the settlements, tall grass on the verges screens everything except the tallest palm trees and the occasional towering evergreen. Wherever the vegetation is low and scrubby, I glimpse the long narrow beach with its grey volcanic sand and lazy rollers fringing the sand with pretty scallops.

Every now and again, there are bars, some just gloomy hovels where a few people have gathered for a bit of shade, but others breezeblock smart with car parks. In the spruce yard of the Escuela de Beverly, tiny navy and white uniformed children as neat as dolls are running about, and nearby a field of delicate chestnut horses stand under trees like glossy statues. Several egrets teeter genteelly amongst them.

Eventually we turn off onto another long, straight but unsealed road, and, just before we are swallowed by 350 square kilometres of banana trees, a large sign welcomes us to Finca Filadelfia.

19 Welcome to the plantation
"Peace, respect and mutual understanding reign in this workplace.
The workers are united. In peace and harmony, we produce quality"

I am yet to read a mission statement that wasn't a lie, a smokescreen or wishful thinking.

We cross a rusty railway line and very soon are surrounded on all sides by row upon row of identical vegetation. Huge coarse mat leaves hang in the still air, brown multi-layered bark sits in brown earth and, every so often, long straight ribbons of blue or brown water lie at the bottom of steep-sided, irrigation channels. As scenery goes, it's poor. As a cash crop or factory farming, it's normal. The mass ranks of monocultures are seldom inspiring and can be depressing, threatening even. But at least in Scotland, when cash crop firs march over the hills, the light is forgiving. Here, the brightness makes it impossible not to feel immediately that the land has been robbed and that everything, except Cavendish bananas and the multinationals they serve, has died.

Bananas are relative newcomers to the Caribbean, although it is thought that humans have been cultivating them since cultivation began. However, the banana as we know it may have originated in Malaysia about 4,000 years ago and about 2,000 years later was carried eastwards to the Pacific and westwards to Africa. It was only after Columbus that Europeans took banana plants to Hispaniola (now Haiti and the Dominican Republic), where the banana was grown as a plantation plant. This would eventually become a staple of the northern developed world until today when the European Union has become the world's largest importer of bananas.

Bananas are undoubtedly one of the wonders of the modern world, growing easily and producing abundantly the year round. For straightforward universal appeal, they have no equal and, while mangoes may be more exciting, they are nowhere near as versatile, nor could they ever be the dietary workhorse the banana has become.

To the majority of shoppers one banana is much like another, as they are all Cavendish, with the choice being between the plantation 'dollar' bananas, which are large and bland, and single farm bananas, which may or may not be organic, and which are always smaller and sweeter. But, in fact, there are hundreds of banana species and none of them are trees but gigantic herbs of the same family as lilies, orchids and palms. The 'trunk' is made up of overlapping, tightly wrapped concentric sheaths, with the true stem or rhizome underground. Above ground, a flowering stalk grows up the centre of the stem and bears yellow flowers that produce bananas in the wild when pollinated by bees or bats (these fruits are inedible as they are very seedy), while cultivated bananas are set without pollination and are seedless and sterile.

Bananas flourish in moist, tropical areas and are grown the world over on a small scale for the domestic market. In most places, they not only eat the raw ripe fruit, but also cook it as a starchy food like potatoes, ferment it to make beer, and use it to make hemp and other building materials. Plants vary from one to nine metres, but growers who supply the North American and European market grow several mutants of the medium height Cavendish that can be planted densely and protected from wind damage but, when grown on plantations, needs vast amounts of agrochemicals. They acquired the Duke of Devonshire's family name in 1836 after he grew them successfully at Chatsworth House, having bought two plants from a collector who brought them from southern China.

Ultimately, it is as an instant food that bananas have conquered the world, being rich in carbohydrates, vitamins C and A, potassium and phosphorous, and for anyone who has lost the will to cook or eat they can be manna from heaven, having no pips, no messy juice and coming wrapped in their own biodegradable wrapper. They are also believed to help with jet lag, constipation and irritable bowel syndrome and, according to a newish theory, eating bananas stimulates the production of dopamine and serotonin, the neurotransmitters which are activated by Prozac and Ecstasy. But these are claims, not my opinion.

After what seems hours but is only minutes, we pull into a clearing. Beside a modest office block and under a shelter open on three sides, a few dozen people in bright yellow aprons and rubber gloves are dipping greens in and out of white tiled pools. Around and about, there are others with cleavers or clipboards. It looks like a film set and the sound system is pulsing with Latino rhythms.

20 Sorting the greens

21 Bathing the greens

22 The Del Monte man

Nobody takes much notice of us, so we wander off down a dusty path between poles strung with nylon cord that is protecting the trees against wind rock. Being medium height, Cavendish are less susceptible to hurricane damage, but they still need protection if they are to crop productively. They flower and fruit only once, but as soon as they are cut they regenerate, and eight months later produce fruit which is ready for picking three months after that.

The air is full of the gentle rustling of plastic. When the trees fruit and the hands reach a certain size, they are covered in a light blue, pesticide soaked bag which keeps them blemish free. It also presents a huge health and disposal problem. In parts of Costa Rica, blue plastic litters the land, clogs streams and rivers and kills any animals who try to eat it. And the same goes for the nylon cord: if it is allowed to lie where it falls, it can sink into the soil so deeply it destroys the structure. 'But not here,' Ben says, pointing to the clear water in the drainage canals.

23 The pesticide-soaked blue plastic bags

24 Drainage canals

Without herbicides, pesticides, fungicides and fertilisers the plantation banana would not crop for long. You don't have to be an agrochemist to know that pests love their food gathered together and that, kept out of balance, nature must be violently overridden. Consequently, Costa Rica, now the second largest exporter of bananas, is a big importer of agrochemicals, many of them banned in the US, and 35% of them are used on bananas.

Several times a month, plantations are sprayed from the air against, among other things, Black Sigatoka, a microscopic fungus that eats away at the leaves and exhausts the plant. Here, I'm told, it is done early in the morning, long before the workers arrive. While it may be possible to protect the workers in theory, it is not possible to protect their water supply or the surrounding land. At least 25% of this spray reaches water and land, and many plantations still use unprotected workers to signal to the planes where to spray.

As a result, many workers suffer from a catalogue of work-related health problems, some life- and livelihood-threatening, others, like sterility, a life sentence. To the multinationals, the work force is often as disposable as the land. They pay subsistence wages, house them in substandard houses and offer no welfare. Workers who make a fuss lose their jobs, as unions are only legal if they are employer-sponsored. If Ticos don't want the jobs, Hondurans can be brought in.

In among the trees, a machete-carrying cutter goes about his business, accompanied by a man with a large, black spongy pad. He is looking for the plants that are market-ready. Then, at some unseen signal, the spongy pad bearer flips it onto the cutter's shoulder and then stands very still and hunched waiting for the machete to slice cleanly through the trunk. Before it hits the ground, he swoops it up and runs with it to the overhead rail while the cutter daubs the cut with fungicide.

'Sometimes snakes sleep in the trees. He can get a bite if he is unlucky,' Ben tells me.

The overhead rail runs all over the plantation. Once the hands are hooked up to it and pieces of yellow foam have been placed between the hard green fruits to stop bruising, one man in a harness hauls them to the processing area. On each journey, he delivers bananas from 25 trees, each one weighing 60 kilos. It looks like the labours of Hercules. They are not big men either, and their small-boned, wiry bodies don't even have massive leg muscles. Yet they haul what must be at least a tonne, several kilometres all day long in the gruelling sun. Some plantations use tractors with wagons, which is more 'advanced' but is costly in fuel, is polluting, and puts people out of work. In the processing area, most of the workers are sitting or standing in rows around conveyor belts or white tiled pools bobbing with greens. A cooling breeze has come up.

25 Hauling the bananas to the processing area

26 Time for processing

When the man hauling the banana train arrives, the hauler removes the sponges and runs off with them for his next job. The hands are immediately chopped down with a short-handled spade and thrown into a long, deep, chemical bath, leaving only a row of stalks, looking like striped green hockey sticks, hanging. Women sort at speed, flinging substandards high into an overhead conveyor that is moving towards a truck, which is slowly filling with rejects for immediate sale in San José. About 15% are rejected. The rest travel on, floating and swirling in and out of pools, on and off conveyors, scales, dryers and graders. Finally, they are individually labelled and packed according to size, blemishes, insect bites and scars.

The premium quality goes for export. Box after plastic-lined box has the air sucked out of it by a machine, is sealed and, just before it is conveyed away for trucking and shipping, a man in a white shirt and beige chinos, with a sheaf of forms on a clipboard, ticks something, gives the nod and they disappear. It's quick; some bananas escape without a single human touching them, and most are handled very little.

On the way out, we stop to look at what looks like sundried snakes but is in fact the composting stalks spread out on the ground, 'giving back the goodness they have taken out,' says Ben, who has quickly grasped what interests me. I smile. It is one tiny compost heap in a huge plantation. It is not going to bring back the forest, revitalise the land and heal the workers.

Yet a world without bananas is hardly thinkable anymore. They have taken over from apples as Britain's number one fruit, and one in every four fruits eaten is a banana. But are we indeed slicing Costa Rica's rainforest onto our cereal?

Many people in Costa Rica think so. Although bananas are extremely important to the economy, so is tourism. Not everyone wants to see the economy grow while land and rivers die. They want a healthy share of the export market but not at any price. So the search is on for the 'ideal' banana; one which travels well and tastes good, yet is capable of protecting itself without such a heavy use of chemicals. Already laboratories select and germinate plants *in vitro* which are so genetically homogenous their ripening date can be predicted to within 48 hours. On plantations, they know before H sails from Belgium which fruits will be ready for his ship. The competition is so fierce that producers have to be able to time the harvest almost to the minute. If they can do this, they surely could also produce a sustainable banana. A tasty banana. One we can eat and be nourished by, without having to wonder what the true price is.

It's good to leave the long, dusty plantation road; to be travelling back among gaudy trees with bright red, orange, or white flowers; to see horses standing as still as death in small fields; to pass the occasional cow and flutter of hens.

Near a stand of cacao trees, the driver suddenly stops. 'Come,' says Ben. He leads me through long, snake-infested grass to a cool aromatic glade hanging with large reddy-yellow, tear-shaped fruit. 'These fruits,' he says picking one, 'have delicious beans. They use them to make chocolate and cocoa.' Each tree is at least four metres, and some have large fruits while others are just beginning to form flowerets. Our driver breaks one open. It is bigger than a coconut and on its way to being a pumpkin. 'Try,' he says smiling for the first time. 'Try the seeds.' He's a big man, strong-boned and muscled but not fat, and with slightly hooded and sympathetic eyes which seem to be carrying some ancient wisdom or suffering. I trust him. The cacao seeds are tangy, thirst-quenching and totally moreish. 'This one will be about five to eight years old,' says Ben, continuing his role as mine of information. 'The trees are cropped twice a year.' 'How does he know all these things,' I wonder. He offers me facts with an ease that only comes from familiarity. And I believe him.

'They're delicious,' I say, sucking enthusiastically, 'much better than a lot of chocolate.'

'Take some with you,' says Ben, as though he owns the place, 'but don't let the farmer see you. He'll shoot you.' Naturally he thinks this is hilarious, but I hurry back to the car with just one stolen fruit for H, wondering why it hadn't occurred to me we were stealing.

Not far from Limón, Ben and the driver suddenly dive for their seat belts. The police are up ahead, talking to people in a Range Rover. Back seat passengers don't need them, but mine is on and, even though it is only a waist job, it's a comfort.

'You've got to watch these police,' Ben says. 'They can be fakes, man. And all they want is to rob you. It's happened a few times along here.' I don't ask how you spot the real thing. But they don't stop us.

Back in Moín the dock is even busier and more hellish-looking and -sounding. Banana-laden trucks are arriving all the time, and I have to pick my way through the noise, litter and people to get to the rickety gangway. At the top, H is paying the sludge man, still egging on the painting gang, and tells me that the bread and the toothpicks have come.

For days, the steward has been on about buying toothpicks in Costa Rica and for days H has been telling him they will come in Europe and that nobody is going to get gingivitis before then. But the Filipino officers have been nagging Juan and, to stop him buying them from his own money, H has ordered a few. They don't like not being able to excavate, which they do enthusiastically after every meal, and think nothing of bullying Juan to whom it has become a crisis. 'Floss is much better anyway,' I told him when I first heard, 'sticks can cause lesions and infections.' Unfortunately, at that point, the third officer sailed into the saloon and, hearing lesions and infections, announced that his wife was a dentist and that sticks were essential. That put the seal on it and he fixed me with one of his winning I-know-best-and-always-will smiles.

This running-out of essentials is a common problem; the fact that the toothpicks were almost finished went unnoticed. And it was the same with the bread, the last slice disappearing into the toaster somewhere near Saint John's. Filipinos call for replacements when they have used the last one. It drives the British mad, but no amount of explaining how essential planning is ever seems to get through. Neither does the fact that most stores and food come in Belgium; emergency rations and local specialities only (mangoes, pineapples, sometimes wine) are bought en route.

It's quite new having to buy bread; before second cooks went (very early in the cutting-to-the-bone programme), bread was always baked on board.

On my first trip, the breakfast table groaned with freshly-baked bread, rolls and scones and, three times a week, the second cook also made wonderful fresh cream cakes and pastries, which were delivered to the bridge for the watch keepers to snack their watches away. In those days (the early nineties), if you wanted to, you could come on board svelte and leave waddling, it took no effort, the food was so delicious and plentiful. Today it's easier to waddle on and leave svelte. That's no bad thing and the food is still very good. But if this drop in standards continues at this rate—and there is every indication it will, as owners and managers feel less and less inclined to make men at sea feel valued—the time may come when it is not only self-service, which it already is on some ships, but self-catering.

Away from the mayhem, on the starboard side, butterflies are resting decoratively on bulkheads and rails and, in the stillness, a delicate golden haze is slowly settling with wispy clouds lying in the gullies between hills which grow greyer and fainter as they rise. As the sun begins to sink, high golden cloud becomes ridged and pink while the dying sun slaps colour on the horizon and a golden pink veil transforms the *Chiquita Scandinavia* and *Cala Piccola* at anchor.

My eye is caught by a rubber dinghy lurking aft between us and the *Pacific Mermaid*. Costa Rica is not a place where drugs are attached to the hull or pirates board, so I am intrigued to see two men climb the slimy vertical steps to the dock to scavenge sheets of discarded cardboard and strips of light blue plastic binding. A woman with a luxurious mop of black bouncy curls tied roughly in a ponytail keeps the dinghy from drifting away while they come and go. The *Pacific Mermaid* has Japanese officers and a Filipino crew, and sources close to our galley have it that several of them have been caught selling drugs in Hamburg and they are not allowed to go ashore in Costa Rica and Colombia. 'They must be mad,' says the third officer, 'risking everything for a few thousand dollars. They will always be marked men,' he adds in the comic book lingo that goes with drug talk.

Getting H away from the ship is a bit like prising a limpet off a rock. And it's not because he isn't keen, but he's always worried about what he might come back to: an accident, a fire in a hold, a strike or worse. No matter how good the others are, it's his head that will roll. So even though he hasn't had time for a sleep, just as it is getting dark, we walk to the gate and pick up a battered old taxi with a bashed-in door and a driver with no teeth we have to wake up.

The Hotel Maribu Caribe is in darkness. The taxi's lights rake the drive as we climb the steep entrance, but there is no sign of life, not a candle, not a torch, nothing. H gropes his way to the front door. It's locked. Puzzled, he gropes back and we shrug and peer into the darkness disappointed. We are very hungry.

When we are sure it is totally dead, we tell the driver to take us to the Matama down the road, eco-tourist spot number two. Unfortunately, he is not an expert three-point turner in a small black space. 'I'm getting out,' I say, after we have twice almost driven into the lobby and three times been near to plummeting over the cliff. When he does finally manage it, he is so happy he sets off at speed, apparently unaware that I am still outside. Fortunately, H is inside the car. Five minutes down the road, lights come on all over the place, but we don't turn back.

At the Matama, they tell us 'the woman who cooks' hasn't arrived. 'Would you like a drink?' says the soft-eyed receptionist in soft-toned English. 'She should come soon. You are very welcome.' It's a beautiful place, not so much a tribal village, more a wildlife park with accommodation. The restaurant, open on three sides, is surrounded by jungle and we look down on a floodlit pool and barbecue. All around, forest paths fan out into nature rambles whose tasteful signs invite us to discover the exotic on our doorstep. Sadly, it is too late and dark for that, but an exquisite cat with golden and white markings is skittering about chasing things that dart, possibly geckos or moths. Slowly, our excitement seeps away into the jungle, as hunger and lack of sleep take their toll.

From time to time, I perk up as monkeys scamper into the light and sit about picking their noses and ears. I also imagine I glimpse the lope of a much larger cat but H, who is yawning and doing his best to look captivated by me and our eco-setting, suggests mildly that hunger may be impairing my otherwise legendary night vision.

Eventually, a waiter wanders by in slow motion, and we persuade him to give us menus we can hardly read it is so dark. Ages later, when he turns up again wreathed in smiles his notebook at the ready, he is surprised and a bit offended that we are standing and pushing in our chairs. 'The barbecue,' he says oozing charm, 'I must cook for the barbecue,' and he points to the pool and a faint glow of coals in a way that suggests either that we are stupid or that we are making completely ridiculous demands on someone already over committed.

'Oh,' we say, sitting down again apologetically, incapable of assertion, 'that's fine, no problem, we had no idea,' but he's off again to serve drinks and get meat sizzling, leaving us to wonder if we will ever get away, let alone eat, and way past calling the evening a treat.

By the time our fish casserole and steak arrive, we feel more like falling into them than using energy eating. It certainly hardly matters that my casserole is watery and served with soft water biscuits, and that I'm starving when I finish, or that H is too tired to tear his steak into edible portions. We are entertained by an American party nearby, describing the wonders of England, particularly the Cotswolds, Devon, Stratford and Warwick Castle, and when one of them says, 'Hey guys ... what about the Highlands of Scotland?' They all say, 'Yeah?' and we perk up an inch or two as she hurls 'amazing', 'awesome', 'stunning' and 'incredible' about, and says, 'and guys, the truly amazing thing was that I had no idea they were even there until I went north of Newcastle.' The Highlands or Scotland, we vaguely wonder.

Not long after we are back on board and are creeping up the stairs, hoping to make the suite undetected and awake, we come face to face with a party of banana luminaries from Colombia. They have dark suits, dark eyes, slick dark hair like straightened snakes and the odour of power oozes from their collective shoulder pads. Among them are the heads of the banana company and the docks, and a retinue of flunkies of important but unspecified rank. I slink away, as though I'm something H has picked up for the night, while he shakes every last hand warmly and offers them coffee, whisky, or Coca-Cola, and they all disappear into hospitality (otherwise known as the conference room). They don't stay long, but it is not because they are concerned that H is bag-eyed because he is doing his job on three hours' sleep. They possibly are too, so that would cut no ice, but they are also probably getting considerably more rewards and heaps more prestige and would consider the very thought of eight hours sleep a grotesque waste.

H is called at 0200—totally unnecessarily as it turns out—to do the port leaving business. From time to time, I half wake thinking we must be at sea, until I notice we are not rolling and there is no thudding in my pillow. At five, I look out blearily and see the crew closing the hatches, the conveyor belts being dismantled and litter strewn everywhere. I get up.

Misty rain veils everything; the bare bulbs of the shed are reflected in puddles, and heaps of bashed in banana boxes are lying in sodden heaps. Among the debris, crows waddle looking like miniature Mother Superiors until they suddenly stab at, and eventually extricate, a piece of blue binding and fly off, strands trailing behind them. A few mangy curs slink and scavenge.

When the light comes, the mist soon lifts from the sea, although the hills are veiled for longer. By the time I organise myself to make my morning coffee and take it to the bridge, the pilot is already there. H is down aft where they are still working. Naturally, he is annoyed at having been called so early, but not with the second officer; the night gang has been very sluggish, which has made working out the leaving time almost impossible. And it's always the same, H says, when he gets back to the bridge.

On the dock below, the dismantled conveyor belts glint in the newly-risen sun. Workers are leaving on bikes, scooters and in old-fashioned buses that lumber towards the gate, all windows open wide. There isn't much movement on the water, just a single pelican cavorting about the bow, and beyond the breakwater, where the surf is rolling in, four figures in yellow waterproofs are trying unsuccessfully to launch a small boat. It is yawing and pitching and refusing to let them jump in.

Just before eight, the *San Jorge* tugs us away from the berth and, out past the breakwater, a noisy dilapidated pilot cutter collects the pilot and takes him to *Chiquita Scandinavia*, which has been at anchor all night. For a short while, butterflies and swifts fly about, and I spot a land bird rather like a finch fluttering about down aft, looking as though she might be taking a ride. At anchor, the *Cala Piccola* has been joined by the *Del Monte Harvester*. What pretty names these reefer ships have. They sound so innocent as though they are trading on behalf of the Garden of Eden.

It's good to be back at sea. Especially in such beautiful weather. After a delicious lunch of Dutch pea soup and tasty sole with a slip down stir-fry, H and self walk up forward so he can inspect the painting job, and we both hang over the side watching the great blue bulbous bow cutting cleanly through the glassy water, and listening to the shish-shish of the gentle wave which is throwing the many flying fish into turmoil. Near the accommodation, he also inspects the onions we are carrying to Colombia. The container couldn't be opened in port for airing, but most are still fine with only one sprouting and a few damp.

There is an infernal racket. The men are scaling the hatch lid under the bridge, their heads covered in dusters.

27 Crew scaling the deck

Several pairs of eyes look up and smile. They are glad to be on deck after all the hatch cleaning below, and they like working together. The dusters are not just to protect them from the burning sun, but to stop it making them too dark (not an asset in Manila). But even in rags they have style; indeed rag-tying is a challenge they rise to every time.

In brilliant sunshine, we are slipping along at full speed, not too far from the coast of Costa Rica, as though on well-greased rollers. Where the luminously deep blue sea meets the slightly lighter sky, the line is sharp and clear except for the odd patch of decorative cumulus. Jed and Beth couldn't be enjoying better cruising conditions for their Panama Canal transit, and I wonder whether they are fighting for rail space to see the locks and the Galliard Cut, and whether Jed is taking against a few more people.

Down aft, the land bird flies up from between the hatch and the accommodation. Eventually, it settles on the aft rail, balancing uncertainly above the churning wake. In flight, it impersonates a tern or a swift (which is probably more to do with battling currents than darting after insects), its browny-black wings flashing white at the tips. On the rail, it swivels constantly, the sun hitting its lovely olive-green head and emphasising the strong finch beak and tan chest. Its long tail is green with a dark tip and it is quite beautiful and, although larger and more colourful than the green finches in my garden, it has their sharp, imperious eye. 'Don't mess with me,' it says, as it teeters.

At sunset, it is still there, a silhouette on the huge fiery ball of the sun. After the sun sinks, flames shoot into the heavens and the bird appears to have massive angelic wings.

'There's a party in the crew bar,' H tells me as I stare into my wardrobe blankly, after my evening soak.

'Whose?'

'The third officer's.' For every birthday, there is a party, and you can't escape on many grounds because, according to the gospel of H, it is in the interest of everyone that we all feel valued, especially on our birthdays. What's more, the doctrine goes on, it raises group morale and maintains confidence in the master.

Never mind that we have to sit with smoke swirling about our heads, watching back-to-back karaoke tapes in which lovelorn Filipina moon about beside the sea, or mooch about on swings in parks, yearning hopelessly. For pre-digested emotions, limp acting and music to puke to, these tapes are without equal.

At eight, when my smiling muscles are already jaded, H tells the third officer he'll do an hour on the bridge for him. The third officer does the eight to twelve watch on here. As it is his birthday, he is very pleased. Freedom for me. 'One hour feeling not just like a fish out of water, but one expected to fly in the sky is enough out of anyone's life,' I chime, as I bound up the stairs past the galley, a sudden rush of energy propelling me effortlessly all the way to the bridge, where I pick up a pile of *Marine Observers*, take them down to the suite and put my feet up.

Birds on ships are always a highlight. Whether they come for five minutes or five weeks, or from the land or the sea, everyone becomes interested to some extent. Even the would-be wits who can't help saying, 'I bet she'll taste good,' are as keen as the rest to help them in their arduous and mysterious transoceanic passages.

The problem is what to do for the best. And this is where the *Marine Observer* is invaluable. It not only publishes extracts from ships' logs of sightings of, say, whales, cloud formations, hurricanes, waterspouts, birds and much more, but it also has tips on identification, as well as how to feed and water them, often with photos. It is an excellent read, whether or not you have a visitor, and at some point on every ship, I devour every copy.

It's put out by the Marine Division of the Meteorological Office. In the days when there were lots of British ships whose bridges were full of cadets and officers of the watch keen to please the master, a first rate report in a log book could end up being selected for publication, and this had cachet.

Unfortunately, Filipino officers are not really scoutish enough to go after nature awards, and it's quite rare for them to get excited about schools of whales or to try to feed skuas who have landed on the bridge wing, let alone painstakingly draw basking moths or exotic butterflies in the logbook. But those who do can earn an Excellent Award for the ship, and a master with enough of these is, or was, presented with a barograph. Photos of barographs being presented, which is possibly an endangered ceremony these days, once appeared regularly in the *Marine Observer*.

H has tried to interest his officers in this slightly extra-curricular activity. After all, observing is part of being an officer of the watch. But he's fighting a losing battle; if he wants a barograph to remind him of all his watch keeping when he retires, he is going to have to buy one.

My initial interest in the *Marine Observer* started when a flock of cattle egrets joined us on a typically balmy passage from Los Angeles to Fiji. They were probably on their way to Hawaii, and couldn't resist the chance to rest. They stayed for about half an hour, teetering comically about the bridge wing while we twitched inside, hardly daring to move in case we scared them off.

And that, we thought, was that, until the next day when, as I sat aft with my morning coffee, two stragglers appeared. Birds don't usually stay long on ships unless they are injured, dehydrated, exhausted or all three. A ship, with its hard surfaces and lack of a food source, is not a sympathetic environment. Yet one of these egrets, which we named Gretel, stayed for weeks (Hansel disappeared after a couple of days), and even when we passed Christmas Island, she made no show of leaving, despite my chasing her about the deck trying to make her fly. Why she stayed was a complete mystery; she may have been tired at first, or perhaps injured although there were no signs. We decided, in the end, she was young and inexperienced, and either confused or seduced by the easy life, as the crew were feeding her.

She finally left in Fiji. Even then, she was in no hurry, but sat on the ship's rail for ages swivelling her beautiful neck as the containers flew above her, apparently watching the shenanigans on the dock. She seemed so reluctant that I began to think she may have lost her nerve or really been injured. A few days earlier, she had flown into a container in the dark and, according to the watchman who heard rather than saw the accident, a pile of white feathers had plummeted into the sea. But later that day she was back in the fo'c'sle strutting about and tucking into prawns and eggs—as recommended by the *Marine Observer* and provided by the galley staff—and flying about as though nothing had happened.

Cattle egrets in the middle of the Pacific seem bizarre, yet the *Marine Observer* had another report with a photo. The really bizarre thing is us: huge islands on the move, perhaps taking them far from where they really want to go.

COLOMBIA: TURBO

When I first look out, the early morning sun is almost covered by a small navy cloud that is casting a ring of gold on the pale, silky water. Moments later, the cloud goes, sunlight shatters on the sea and the air is a wash of golden light, which makes hills shimmer, hard ridges soft and the distant coffee-growing mountains faint lines so high they could be clouds.

Down aft there is no sign of the bird on the dewy deck, but the crew's footsteps are everywhere; they are emptying the lifeboats and removing anything from the decks that isn't a fixture. Once the banana trains arrive, everything is up for grabs. 'It's all opportunistic,' says H, 'so keep the door locked all the time whether you are in or out.'

We are in the Golfo de Urabá, gateway to the Colombian banana belt, which pushes deep into the western end of the country's long Caribbean coast. On the eastern side, behind a spit of land—Punta de las Vacas—lies the lawless Turbo. Few tourists come here, and those that do soon move on.

No one has a good word to say for Turbo; as dollar banana ports go, they don't come any worse. A few trips ago, while the captain was at dinner, intruders broke down his door and emptied the safe. But that could—and does—happen everywhere. In Antwerp, for example, one captain was drugged as he slept. But in Turbo, it is not just a question of robbery. One time, there was a party on board for the office staff and only half of them turned up. The other half had been gunned down in their downtown office, minutes before they were due to leave. Ironically, it was the party that saved the survivors; the gunmen intended to kill them all.

'The killing fields of Urabá', is how Colombia's great banana producing region has been described, but the struggle for control of the wealth of this spectacular region is not being fought with words in Bogotá, or even at the World Trade Organisation in Geneva. Here, people have been dying for decades, and today violence against banana workers is routine; thousands have been forced off their land and nobody knows exactly how many have been killed, caught between the right-wing paramilitaries and the left-wing guerrillas. In the name of the large landowners, paramilitaries get rid of workers who try to organise to improve their conditions, and left-wing guerrillas kill workers who appear to toe the paramilitary line.

In Turbo, we don't go alongside; all the loading is done at anchor, not because it is dangerous, but because the bay is too shallow. Normally, when we load at anchor, liberty boats—as they are called as though we were in prison—take us ashore, but here we are not advised to go unless we have a bodyguard. So the bananas come to the ship in floating trains which look at a distance like flat wriggling worms snaking across the head of the gulf. They are in fact docks and barges called zungos and bongos which are loaded in the plantations and towed down the River Leon, bongos carrying the bananas and zungos the galley, the food, cooks, generators and anything else needed to maintain an army of stevedores, guards, and overseers.

During the loading, we are locked in, and only the overseers have access to the accommodation. There are captains who open their ship, and there was a time when sex workers came with the barges and climbed through the window into the crew bar. Now they say they do their business in the zungos, if they come at all, which they don't on this charter. Or if they do, they are very secretive, and certainly no one from the ship has been seen going down the gangway whistling idly and trying not to look furtive. So it is possibly a thing of the past, not because of a new age of moral rectitude, or even because anyone is heeding the safe sex videos, but because the crews are so small that if they are not working they are sleeping.

The gulf is several miles wide. As we manoeuvre about a mile from the Punta, waiting for the authorities to clear the ship, misty mountains rise and fall to port, tiny settlements dot the coast with forested hills behind, and where the land is bare it glows red in the morning sun. As the sun climbs, the ridges sharpen and dark shadows lie in the valleys. There are gannets about and fishing boats near the coast and, eventually, a tiny boat carrying the authorities noses round the Punta and slowly grows as it ploughs laboriously towards us.

Clearing the ship is a strange ritual which owes a lot to tribalism and varies only in detail from place to place. No conciliatory dancing is required these days, but offering small gifts—which they consider their due—is essential to ensure things go smoothly. First up the gangway is the tall and patrician agent. He nods and smiles. Behind him, their heads down as though en route to the scaffold, thud a couple of khaki-uniformed persons, then a posse from the cast of *The Godfather,* whose muscles are escaping from their short-sleeved shirts, and whose black hair is glinting with cream. As they rush by, as though being pursued by pit bulls, they leave a stream of pungent aftershave so strong the air is almost unbreathable. Some manage a muttered *buenos días*, one shakes my hand and they are all clutching large leather bags.

They are from the Port Authority, Immigration and Health, and are here to check our intentions (bananas), identities (passports), and health (inoculation certificates, especially the dengue fever ones). The bags are for the complementary gifts—swag to you and me—and, when they have been filled, they sign us clear, sit back and ask H a few polite questions about his family and the trip, and leave.

The next launch has the guards: all Hispanics and all uniformed and armed. They rope off no-go areas and stand at strategic places (near the gangway, up forward, down aft and down hatches), looking try-hard mean but puny beside the blacks. Occasionally they twiddle their elongated truncheons, which hang at their sides like extra members. My smiles of welcome are met with blank stares and, although after a while they give a little, I make a mental note not to take my hands out of my pockets too quickly. Their job is to keep order and make sure no unauthorised persons board with the intention of stowing away or depositing large amounts of cocaine in gratings. They are frequently unsuccessful on both counts.

The last launch brings the pilot and we set off for the winter anchorage at the head of the gulf in the Bahía Colombia.

'I knew when I saw the captain that he have his wife,' the pilot says, shaking my hand and bowing slightly when H introduces me. 'He looks happy. You women are everything to a man ...' I smile the smile of one who knows flannel with a subtext when she hears it (if you're not everything, then why not), and he smiles back warmly. He is not insincere; he really means it. 'Starboard twenty ... see these eyes,' the pilot nods towards H who is glowing like a live coal, 'how they are full of happiness. Me, now, I am away from my wife and family. They are in Barranquilla altogether and I am in Turbo miserable.' He pronounces every syllable of miserable in case we are thinking this small talk.

'I used to be in the Colombian Navy,' he says proudly. 'I had my own ship,' and he produces a photo of himself as *el capitano* heavily striped with British Navy epaulettes. (H wears these same epaulettes, not the regular Merchant Navy ones; an honour bestowed on the Blue Star Line in recognition of the many ships and men they lost in both world wars.) An eagle sits on his gold-heavy cap with something else which he explains but which I immediately forget. British Navy epaulettes are still one of the world's desirable pomps, apparently. Wear them and swank.

A small boat crosses our path—there are quite a few about, but when the pilot blows the whistle, it disappears in a cloud of spray. He blows again, when a banana train blocks the fairway between two ships, but it doesn't move, so he alters, skirting the *Winter Sea*, the *Fuji Star* and the *Osaka Bay*, all already anchored and busy loading. As we slow down, our cranes, hatches, and the bridge wings become festooned with the now familiar Day-Glo-striped monster butterflies. Pelicans are about too, lumbering through the air in packs looking thuggish.

'I am five years in the Navy in Barranquilla,' says the pilot, proudly producing a picture of his retirement party. 'Now I live a double life.' He sighs. 'In Barranquilla, everything is luxury with a big shiny car, very good clothis and perfumes, but here I must wear these clothis,' and he pulls at his very smart, pale yellow shirt with a cream stripe and his well-cut expensive-looking chinos. They are not the style statement of a frump on the bread line and I wonder what language his Barranquilla clothis speak. I smile sympathetically, which prompts him to say (for some inexplicable reason), 'You look very rich. You must earn a lot of pounds.' The wheelman's shoulders twitch. His English is good. It will all go back to the crew, who love to hear stories of our living in luxury. We show them pictures of Lismore with restraint, otherwise they start to imagine we are impossibly wealthy, mistaking a croft with panoramic views of the Sound of Mull, for a ranch. Why they imagine H would be delivering bananas if we were ranched is a mystery.

As we come close to the anchorage, the pilot suddenly runs on his short legs from the port to starboard and back again shouting, 'Stop engines ... dead slow ahead ... dead slow astern,' then, after one more dash which is more like a dance, he inspects his parking from all angles, raises his arms, and crosses them to indicate that we are done and says, 'Perfecto! Let go the anchor, Captain—four shackles in the water.'

Not long after we are securely shackled, the first tugs arrive carrying what look like several basketball teams, i.e. very tall, fit-looking bodies carrying sports bags. Like Limón, Urabá has a large black population, descendants of slaves who settled the jungle-fringed coasts and riverside towns. When they spot me on the bridge wing, where I am looking through the binoculars at our miniature banana train just coming into the bay from the river, they blow kisses, whistle and generally carry on as though they are a fully-warmed-up television audience responding to a cue card. On the main deck, the crew are preparing the cranes and opening the hatches and, in no time, the decks are swarming with hip-swinging, flesh-pressing, good-looking workers.

By mid-morning, the world is a furnace and we are surrounded by reefers with banana trains trailing away from their sterns and zungos nestling into their hulls. Everywhere, cranes are swooping and swinging and towers of palleted banana boxes in slings are making slow arcs in the stifling air. Above them, sweating crane drivers pull levers and peer down, guiding them into the holds.

28 Uncovering the banana boxes on the bongo

29 Bongos arriving

30 Loading begins

31 Stowing the banana boxes

32 The catering zungo

Near the gangway on the starboard side, the long catering/entertainments zungo has been nudged into position by a very battered and rusty tug. Round a large wooden table, the tug drivers are at a poker school. Slightly hunched with their legs wide, they slap cards down and sweep them up, smoke billowing about their heads and weedy-looking, well-sucked fags between their yellow fingers. Occasionally they all whoop and wave their arms about.

Most of the zungo is a gloomy looking galley with a part-tin and part-tarpaulin roof, under which I can just make out a few tables and chairs. Near the entrance, a huge hunk of some beast, perhaps a bullock, is steeping in a large plastic drum. Beside it, a wizened man is assembling banana boxes, laboriously painting them with glue and slowly disappearing as they pile up around him. Unlike him, they will travel the world. A constant procession comes and goes from the galley, and they all stop to watch him work, as small crowds like to watch men working in holes on the road or on building sites.

Our banana train is tied up to port, with three bongos being worked by three cranes. When the loaded pallets fly into the hold, four men leap up, catch them and guide them into place, releasing the slings which fly free like demented birds. Swiftly and rhythmically, the stackers pack the boxes, with or without accommodation for stowaways.

This is, or can be, where illegal boarders make their entrance. It is here that stevedores in the know, with minimum fuss and maximum inducement, can arrange the boxes, leaving body-sized spaces for one, two or even more couriers to live in enormous discomfort, having cold air blown over them for our two-week return journey. They are not put off either by the very long knife which an authorised stowaway detector—a shoresider—plunges into every stack in every hatch before we leave. But the word is they know where not to poke these knives. Certainly, I am yet to hear tales of bloodcurdling screams or of blood covered bananas at the other end.

Late afternoon, in the cooling breeze, H and self go for a stroll around the deck, and he offers our old mattress to the first person we meet who, unable to believe his ears, flies up the outside stairs and teeters drunkenly down several flights, the mattress on his head. When it is safely on the zungo, he pats it several times, as though it were a dog, and calls out that he is *mucho contento* (by about ten).

Near number one crane, the second engineer, the chief officer and the lecky are discussing, yet again, why it is still leaking oil. 'She like me,' says the lecky, sniffing, 'too old.' Suffering is writ large on his pale and drawn face. During the night, his temperature has been high, he is aching all over, and has no energy. 'When I am well, I think I am young man,' he tells me. 'When I am sick, I know I am old man,' and he laughs pitifully.

'You should be in bed,' I say, before I can stop myself, immediately remembering the time an Egyptian visitor writhed in my flat for a whole day, screaming and cursing and speaking in tongues, and reducing me to emotional rubble, when all he had was indigestion. And afterwards, everyone said, 'Oh they always go on like that,' as though I were the only one who didn't know about this other side of the stiff upper lip syndrome.

'Bed!' says the lecky, as though I have said something outlandish and can have no idea what it is to be burdened by a pneumatic crane with an oil leak. 'Work. Must work,' and he throws his ailing arms high and shuffles off.

There are even more butterflies flashing green and gold in the unforgiving sun, and the occasional large dragonfly or damselfly hovers and darts on lurex wings finer than any lace. But there are no seabirds, just one crow-like creature hopping clumsily about the cranes, and far off, a heron is flapping slowly towards the mangroves.

From up forward, where the only sound is the pale-faced puny guard pacing among the ropes, we look down onto the main deck. It's meal time for one gang, and they are gathering round two large aluminium pots, one with meat, the other rice. After a quick rummage in their sports bags for bowls, they help themselves and then lounge about laughing and joking. Suddenly one of them stands up and immediately falls flat on this face. Someone has tied his laces to a pallet.

Maddened, he pulls a knife from his pocket, unties his laces, and then goes from person to person, grabbing at any clothing they are wearing, which isn't much, the knife poised. 'Cripes,' I say appropriately, hastily putting away my camera and looking round at the guard whose impassive face is staring out to sea, as though he is on another planet or in a deep meditation. H says nothing, but I move closer to his slightly stiffened body planning to go behind it if needs be.

The knife-bearer is a small Hispanic, and I would have thought no match for the giant blacks, but eventually he has one of them on his back, the knife in the air at which point I look away, assuming I am dreaming. I have never knowingly seen anyone stabbed and I am not about to spoil that.

'What sort of a job is this?' I stage screech into H's sweating back. 'We're just out for a gentle stroll, minding our own business and we're surrounded by madmen. What's happening? Tell me what's happening?'

'You walk back down the other side.' H says quietly. 'I'll follow.' But I am gripped or possibly frozen and remain attached to his back, my eyes closed. H calls the guard, who takes his time, and when I open my eyes, the attacker is throwing his victim down and slinking back to his food and everyone is eating normally.

As we stroll back past them with studied casualness, they all smile at H nod at me and say '*Esposa del capitán?*' as though butter wouldn't melt, and I smile weakly, not knowing the Spanish for bit on the side.

Near the gangway, we meet the beaming mattress man who is loudly promising us all the mangoes we can eat next time. Just as I am assuring him I not only like but have no self-control around mangoes, a launch draws up and a small fat man in a white jumpsuit two sizes too small is leaping about and gesticulating wildly, looking very like Pavarotti on a run up to a high note. H waves and tells me he is the foreman and the next thing a minion is beside us with a huge bag of ground coffee and an even huger jar of Nescafé. Beans would have been better, we both think ungraciously, as we wave and mouth our thanks.

When darkness comes, and all the ships and trains light up and the mangroves and land disappear, I stand near the gangway beside the guard, wondering who is the more dangerous: the armed or the unarmed. Below me, on the catering zungo, those who have finished for the day are waiting to leave. Some are cleaning their teeth, hands and armpits; one is riding a small collapsible bicycle round and round as though he is in a circus; a studious type is reading something about philosophy; the poker school is still going; a potential Mr Colombia is posing on a stage made from flattened banana boxes, muscles rippling and knotting as he plays his body like a musical instrument; and the rest are eating, sleeping, or just mooching.

Occasionally, someone calls up that he wants my shoes, my tee shirt, my jeans, and the rest look up vaguely interested in what might come of it. There is a constant procession up and down the gangway but no sign of any zungo girls.

Before we sail from the working anchorage at ten o'clock, the head security man tells H that one potential stowaway has been taken away in handcuffs.

'Where was he planning to hide?' H asks.

'Don't know, Sir. We caught him first.'

'What will happen to him?'

'It depends whether he has tried it before. If he hasn't, he will spend three days in custody in the naval base here. If he has he will be sent to Medellin for ...' and he wiggles his hand about in the air meaning 'who knows'. 'It is not such a nice place.' He laughs feebly. 'It is not like a Belgian prison.' He also says that he's sure there won't be any stowaways or drugs this trip. The big boys are not using these reefers any more—they have switched to planes and submarines via Caribbean islands they can control more easily—and, most of all, the small people, the chancers, are temporarily scared off by all the publicity, which possibly means they will try even harder to get the crew to be couriers.

Being asked to carry drugs is part of coming to Colombia. The crew are usually offered about $1000 per kilo and, naturally, some are tempted, although no one has ever been caught on here. Unfortunately, doing it once means you are marked, owned and forever exploitable, which may explain why one terribly normal deck fitter suddenly lost the plot in Costa Rica and threatened to break both his arms if he wasn't allowed off. And he meant it; he was terrified of setting foot in Colombia and although H concluded it was a bad case of courier fever, the fitter denied it vehemently. Naturally.

The leaving pilot is a quiet fatherly sort who peers from horn-rimmed spectacles and gives the bridge an air of calm and gentility. He is from Cartagena and is quick to tell us he does not enjoy the time he spends in Turbo. 'There is no respect for life,' he says, which seems an understatement. 'Everyone is, I think you say, on the make. They come to your ship and they want something; whisky, coke, cigarettes, anything as long as it is costing nothing. And if they cannot get anything, then they try to steal. Me, I want only water from ships. We haven't had any rain and we don't expect any, maybe for two or three months at least.'

When we anchor again off Punta de las Vacas, the pilot and all the guards, now dressed in civvies and carrying their sports bags, file down the gangway, and the agent with the authorities troops up. The port leaving business is done quickly, but we can't sail; all ships leaving Colombia have to have their hulls searched. Welding tubes onto banana boat rudders and filling them with drugs is not unknown and, although the chief officer and second engineer do a drug and stowaway search before leaving every port, they are not expected to dive.

The night is like a large warm overcoat when the divers finally arrive an hour late, saying their propeller was caught in a fishing net, and they didn't think they would make it at all. Spotlit in the beam of the bridge light, the head diver stands on his small boat and does a slow strip, his legs wide, his chest expanded as though our decks are full of adoring muscle heads. When he's down to his briefs, he does a quick posing routine, various bits bulging and deflating in quick succession, his admiring eyes following them with the odd coy glance up to his invisible audience. Eventually, he signals to the other two—who have changed modestly in the shadows and are waiting patiently—and they plop over the side like three pebbles. For forty-five minutes, the only sign of them is the occasional little trail of bubbles which catch the light as they travel from forward to aft. If it were daylight we would be flying the A flag, signalling to other ships that we had divers down. In the blackness, flag signals are not useful.

'Nothing found, Sir,' says stripper when they are all in the office ready to sign the 'nothing found' certificate in triplicate, each with a bottle of beer and Coca-Cola.

They are fit-looking bodies with action man's hard, muscled legs and arms, and nipped in waists. They are not particularly tall yet they fill the room, the head man sitting in front of the desk and the other two standing near the door, their legs splayed to accommodate diver's thighs. 'You are lucky today, Sir; tomorrow there will be no bananas to load.' H smiles, but doesn't speak. 'A man, a very, very big man, is shot today and there will be no fruits tomorrow. The people don't work today picking.' He shrugs. 'Turbo is a dangerous place. Dangerous for everyone, and especially for me.' Like everybody else, he talks in generalities. Drugs, bananas, whatever the root of the violence, there's no distinction made. It's just part of living in Turbo. 'I am a straight diver and I do my job straight, but two years ago I find a lot of drugs on one ship and after that my life is threatened. But that was when the drugs capital was Medellin and now it is Cali and they are more clever and they don't just go round killing. They are too smart for that.'

'If it's so dangerous,' says H, 'why do you do it?'

'Someone must do it,' he says with a shrug, as though he is altruism on well-developed legs. 'But it is not so bad now. They are not using these ships, but planes and sometimes submarines. There was one in Santa Marta pretending to show tourists the sea-life, but really it was taking the drugs out.' H is yawning. The night is wearing on, and he is anxious to be an officer who is well-rested before our next port, Santa Marta. The divers take the hint. 'It's late sir,' he says signing the necessary and standing up to go.

By daylight, we are sailing in perfect conditions along the Caribbean coast of Colombia towards Santa Marta in the west. The sun is up, visibility is exceptional and an archipelago is scattered off Punta San Bernardo as though some celestial cook has flung the ingredients of a golden cake about. Mid-morning the coral islands, reefs and lagoons of the Corales del Rosario drift by, many so small they are mere dots on the blue, but on others I can see the obligatory sun-drenched sands and palm trees waving with holiday brochure abandon.

For most of the morning, the mainland coast comes and goes, a faint undulating line on the horizon, with no sign of settlements until the tall buildings of Cartagena appear. As we get nearer, the Colina de la Popa, the highest point in the city, rises sharply and the white walls of the Convento de la Popa and an illuminated cross on its summit catch the sun and wink erratically. (These things are marked on the chart, and for the first time I understand why they are called landmarks.) Beneath it, the spires and domes of the old city of Cartagena nestle and shine, and then the modern high rises spread out along the coast.

Cartagena has the largest and most secure natural harbour on the entire coast, plus an inner harbour near the town and a famous naval base. Ahead, two smart-looking warships, one much bigger than the other, appear to be coming straight for us and the third officer is worried. 'Every time I alter, they alter,' I hear him tell H on the phone, 'they are playing with our lives.' Fortunately they tire of it and steam off, but not before they have tested all the third officer's knowledge of who gives way to whom and when, and wasted a good deal of H's time. Still it confirms H's opinion that the third officer knows the rules of the sea, which is a great relief, and not always the case with a third officer.

Cartagena is a walled city, the second the Spanish established, Santa Marta being the first. But, unlike Santa Marta, much of the old city survives, partly because Cartagena was one of the places where they kept the stolen riches until they could get them back to Spain. This made it a target of any number of pirates, among them Sir Francis Drake, who besieged it in 1586 and only agreed not to burn it down after they paid him 10 million *pesos*, which he promptly shipped back to England. Ironically, it was because the city was so often under attack that they fortified it so well. And it is intact today because they were defending not just the plundered gold, but a gateway into the colonised interior.

Around lunchtime, the high buildings of Barranquilla are beginning to sprawl about the mouth of the mighty Río Magdalena a mere eight miles away, and mid-afternoon, we round Punta Faro where the mangrove-covered coast sweeps inland and we alter for Santa Marta. Almost immediately, the wind gets up, and a short time later, the murky, woolly outlines of the great mountains poke their peaks over the horizon, like a monster from the deep that sharpens and darkens as it rises.

'There are beautiful beaches here,' the third officer says, dressed in his spotless white boiler suit, ready to go forward for stations (tying the ship up), and waving his arm at the golden sands smiling generously on either side of the first tower blocks poking out of the mouth of the bay. When Santa Marta appears dead ahead, the tower blocks of the very popular resort of El Rodadero, slowly move to starboard, while away to port the magnificent mountains, soaring behind the town, swoop slowly down to the coast towards the Isla de la Aguja.

33 Santa Marta from the sea

COLOMBIA: SANTA MARTA

Sailing into the Bahía Santa Marta is extremely picturesque. The town stands on a quite narrow plain, mountains rising up behind it and all around. High up with the clouds and mist, are the peaks of the great Sierra Nevada de Santa Marta, the highest chain in Colombia, while in front, right behind the port, the Cerro San Quemado or Pico de Santa Marta are covered in parched earth and cacti bushes.

Outside the bay, the pilot boards from a smart cream, red and black cutter. Close by, pelicans are clustered on the calm green water, while further out, where the water turns blue and rough with a sharp line like a tide rip, hundreds of seabirds are boisterously feeding, rising and falling like breaking waves. The pilot boards very near the Morro Grande, a rocky outcrop with precipitous sides and a large white lighthouse beneath which several small fishing boats are bobbing about. In the calm waters further in, tourists are sheltering under the brightly-striped awnings of small sightseeing craft, but there is no sign of the sneaky drug submarines pretending to tour.

Although he isn't young, the pilot climbs the ladder athletically, shaking my hand and saying 'welcome' as he passes briskly through the bridge wing, drops his bag on the chart table and immediately begins to pad about, his expensive-looking deck shoes squeaking loudly.

'Santa Marta looks beautiful from the sea,' the lecky says, as we gaze at a picture book town where a white-domed cathedral is nestling amongst medium- or low-rise buildings, where palms are waving and colourful buses are buzzing along the seafront, and where people are swimming or sitting about under bright splashes of umbrellas. 'But when you walk there ... well ... it is really nothing.' He laughs his resigned laugh, as though he has just defined human existence. The fatal flaw. Nothing survives intense scrutiny. 'Nothing,' he repeats, in case I hadn't quite got the idea. 'But the mountains. From the sea, they are wonderful.' He shrugs and walks away. Nothing beats the Adriatic, his back tells me, with a bit of "why-am-I-here" thrown in. As the town moves nearer, I can just make out a huge fading ad for Kent cigarettes on the side of an ageing building.

The *Chiquita Elke* and a cool carrier, the *Hausa Stockholm*, are already tied up as we move into the berth, and behind them are scrubby, ridged, dry brown hills.

34 Tied up in Santa Marta, ready to load

A grain silo, festooned with constantly-strutting pigeons, dominates the dock, and a large statue of the Virgin Mary, in celestial blue with the baby Jesus in her arms, stands on the hill above the sea, their golden haloes glinting in the sun. From time to time, clouds of pigeons whoosh into the air and swoop over the land. On the water, darting, chattering swifts and giant butterflies join the pelicans.

Berthing in Santa Marta is tight. There is only one huge tug, the smart cream and red *Barranquilla*, plus the anchor to stop us suddenly swinging round and demolishing the quay or knocking over the huge grain portainer. As we creep nearer, the pilot gets more and more agitated and theatrical, rushing frenetically from wing to wing, leaning over and measuring, calling and waving wildly, with H following, pouring a stream of balm over his turbulent outbursts. Every now and again, for no reason I can see but perhaps just before his heart fails, the pilot suddenly stops, as though despair has overtaken him, his stricken face saying, 'Oh I am troubled and it will all end in tears.'

35 Berthing in Santa Marta

During one of these sudden halts, he raises his arms, utters a cry from his depths, buries his head in his hands and paces back and forth saying 'Oh my God,' or its equivalent, before rushing on again. Then, to my horror, he notices me and stops again, turning his back on the entire show, bowing theatrically, a sad little smile trying to find a home on his face. This is so alarming I grin feebly and run, worried that during one of these polite bows the unattended vessel may indeed demolish the quay and my presence, albeit far back on the bridge wing where no one could accuse me of being 'in the way', will be cited as the cause. 'The captain's wife was on the bridge, my Lord,' I hear them say at the inquiry. 'The captain's wife you say? On the bridge! Is that normal Mr. Pilot?' and for Captain's wife the court will hear siren extraordinaire, and know that at least I was propositioning them all, while being in the fairway and obstructing every view.

Before I disappear altogether with this doom-laden scenario, I hear H say, 'They are going as fast as they can,' and as they both hurl themselves the length of the bridge once more, H adds 'But the rope will break, Pilot.' Later he tells me the pilot wanted the headline wound in more quickly and that the second officer could do no more. He also says we were in no danger of destroying the portainer and that he was a good pilot and one of the calmer ones.

'Calmer! I had to leave. Warn me when you get a highly strung one.'

The docks are extremely clean and every square inch is covered with hordes of uniformed boys and girls lounging about waiting for the ship to be cleared. Without exception, they are young, very neat and so full of life they look as though they may break into a chorus of 'I love to go a stevedoring', standing tall and smiling in their blue tee-shirts, grey shorts, and blue hard hats. The mooring gangs are also uniformed, but in green shirts and khaki shorts, and in amongst all this, brightly painted trucks with latticework sides, bright canvas tops and sparkling grillwork are lined up, full of bananas.

It's a colourful, festive scene, more tropical musical than banana port, and even the boys in khaki with very large weapons, overdressed for the heat in the not-so-appealing army brown, with big black boots, lemon squeezer hats turned up at one side and black straps under their boyish chins, look like actors. Indeed, their angelic faces are so unthreatening they may have just come from making their first communion. And even the guard high up in a sentry box, his gun at the ready, looks as though he could not possibly know what a bayonet was for.

The authorities take their time, but eventually they pile out of a couple of yellow taxis and lumber slowly up the gangway, their flesh wobbling in slow motion and making the gangway swing. One of them shakes my hand and almost rips it off; another peers over his glasses, his large stomach unpleasantly brushing my flat one, as he glowers as though he is deciding whether a biological specimen is poisonous. Then he smiles and laughs. He's figured out who I am and he isn't going to have me shot. We shake hands and both laugh for ages. I've brought out the family man in him. Then H comes along and we all laugh a bit more.

'He probably thought you were a provedore,' H explains later. 'They don't like people coming onto the ship before they do. They don't like it at all. And pushy provedores they particularly hate.'

As soon as the authorities are off, pretty boys with bayonets are posted at the top of the gangway, and an almost stationary queue of jocund youths snakes up, having their bags and IDs checked. Occasionally someone is turned away or a bag is thrown down to the quay. Meanwhile the onions are being landed, and then the cars come up one by one in an open-sided steel platform, which swings through the air and lands on the quay. As they are revved up and driven away, the ship's dust is wiped from the windscreen by brand new wipers. They are off to a dealer in Bogotá, and the drivers seem keen to enjoy their brush with refined, expensive auto thrust.

'I would say zis is San Tropez for the Colombians,' says Nicole the provedore, down to try and sell H what he has no intention of buying. She is beautiful. Exquisite, even. And she has a thankless task. 'But zen, I am French.' She is sitting opposite H, assuring him he need look no further for his provisions, her eyes (Bambi, but efficient) saddened to hear that he has bought all he needs in Moín. She speaks very good English but with that accent which makes everything sound like foreplay.

'But surely there is somezing for za bond—cigarettes, wheesky? And here is somezing for your wife.' I'm on my way upstairs and have been called in to meet her. She hands me a photocopied map with Santa Marta's attractions highlighted.

'Is it safe to walk about?' I say studying the map, which recommends shopping, discos and restaurants, but makes no mention of lost cities, the very famous Tayrona National Park, indigenous people or museums full of relics from ancient civilizations.

'Oh yes,' she purses her lips perfectly. I must practice that, I think, hoping she will do it again. No one could ever wish to harm the bearer of such cute lips. 'But near the gate it is danjeruse. There are robbers in this part and if you walk it is danjeruse but in a taxi no.' More fetching lip shapes. 'In the town you can walk about no problem.'

'And to eat?' says H.

'For eating, I would say there is only one place really, the Pan Americano, here,' and she points to it on the map and to her underlined recommendation. 'That is the best place, unless you want to go to Rodadero, which is much, much better. Ya, much better for shopping, deesco, eating etc. And now it is the holiday, so it is very good there.

Wonderful. But if you want to stay in Santa Marta,' and her tone implies that only a partially braindead blob would, 'then the Pan Americano has the best food, and it is air conditioned. In fact, it is so air conditioned it is cold and you will need somezing to be warm,' and she laughs and hugs herself and says, 'I was zere the other night and I was very cold.'

H orders cigarettes because he feels sorry for her, not because he believes her seductive beams mean she thinks he's a real stud. But he is the man with the stripes holding the purse strings. And a successful provedore has to tug them open, whatever it takes.

The agent arranges a car to get me out of the docks. I'm doing well on here; in most places, the days when the captain's wife was whisked away in a limo—with or without the captain—and given a tour with lunch thrown in, are well gone. In fact escaping alive from docks is one of the great trailing challenges wherever you are. Docks are hazardous especially for pedestrians. If you are not in danger of being demolished by flying containers or rampaging juggernauts, as in Singapore, for example, miscreants will be after your cash, your passport and/or your life. And, as a woman, just being on a dock means you are a lowlife of some sort. Many pairs of eyes will tell you so.

As though to prove my point, the young man on duty at the gate with the huge gun looks at my pass, at me, at my pass, and again at me several times before he nods me through, his young eyes flooded with indifference mixed with doubt. The captain's wife, eh? He's seen it all. Or learned to look as though he has. Around him, several heavily-armed, bored young men are either kicking the dust absently, or larking about in groups, or standing alone and staring vacantly. Just beyond the gate, a shifty-looking crowd without guns or uniforms are lounging with no obvious intent around taxis, lots of parked scooters and a few unappealing-looking food stalls. I get a taxi and, away from the gate, the road becomes deserted and bleak—the really dangerous bit—and in two minutes, we are in the happy pulsing holiday town.

Santa Marta is not a foreign tourist town, so I am not surprised when the driver takes no notice when I ask him in Spanglish to let me out. Instead, he says something that sounds like rapid gunfire and drives on pointing at statues, buildings or beaches leaving me with no option but to settle back and hope that I have not been kidnapped. Colombia is, or was, the kidnapping capital of the world, although captains' wives are not a known target, which is just as well, because paying ransoms is forbidden by law here, which can mean that hostages moulder for months and years in caves and huts in one of the many out-of-the-way sierras and deserts.

The streets are busy. Colombians from everywhere else are here on holiday, and are either standing on their horns or coming out of side streets—without stopping—in huge four-wheel drives, and screaming to a halt behind little crammed buses. There is a lot of swerving, near misses and shouting, but no ugly, stale rage erupting after years of suppression. Here, the wild theatricality is fresh, naked impatience—they do not appear to be spoiling for a murder.

When we leave the deeply unappealing-looking seaside bars and reasonably-appealing beach stalls, we whizz through the dusty, scruffy outskirts where children are playing in front of low cave-like, garishly painted breezeblock houses covered in grills. Every now again in the general dilapidation there is something ugly but smart, covered from top to bottom in glossily painted grills. Even the roof tiles are grilled. It must be strange to live with such total distrust. In Lismore, you really can go out and leave your door open for as long as you like. Just don't leave your whisky visible. Or so the joke goes.

My attempts to get the driver off the main drag are futile, and we soon join the jumble of out-of-control buses, pickups, cars and taxis hurtling, many on the wrong side of the road, over the hill to El Rodadero. 'Rodadero,' the driver says, bursting with pride as we reach the top of the hill and begin our descent, having swerved past two or three giant hoardings and almost everything else on the road.

Lovely,' I say. 'Super,' I add quickly, seeing him want more and even turn to get it, which is chilling in this madness. 'Very nice indeed,' I say very clearly, as I gaze down at a forest of tower blocks plonked in front of the sea. It looks like a beach film set, with lower rise luxury apartments gathered together on the outskirts, looking aloof, and seriously rich behind their cream facades and neoclassical porticos.

36 Santa Marta from the Rodadero road

The town is busy; there is not a square inch to be had on the beach, cars line all the streets, people swim in the polluted water, shop in the smart new shopping centres, drink in the cafés and bars, and stroll about with not much on, looking incredibly beautiful and alarmingly self-conscious. They all seem to have sprung from the same set of genes and there is not a dumpy, stocky, triple-chinned, shambling gait to be seen.

Viewed through the taxi window, it is so depressing I lose all desire to get out. Here I am, having faced elemental dangers day after day, and my reward is something so un-different from many other apparently wealthy resorts, inertia creeps over me from the feet up and walking isn't an option.

Round the back of the town where new flats are still going up on waste ground, the driver gets out and beckons me to follow. 'Deesco,' he beams as though he has discovered the source of the Nile, and we cross a pleasant bridge over an unremarkable man-made lake. 'La Escollera,' he adds, pointing to the sign, and I follow him into what feels at first like a church— all hush and darkness you have to adapt to before you can see anything.

It's deliciously cool. The attractive wooden dance floor is surrounded by monastic flagstones with monastic tables and chairs made from what look like ancient hardwoods. Above is a gallery with more seating under a thatched roof hanging with large ethnic wicker baskets. Near a stage full of plants with a waterfall and abandoned instruments, two men—in black fishnet shirts (from which grizzly hair is escaping) and wearing massive medallions and expensive, tight trousers—are in a conspiratorial huddle. The nauseating smell of stale smoke is overlaid with cloying aftershave. I ask if I can snap them and their deesco. Without uttering a word, they fling their tooled leather shoulder bags about their fishnets, look at me with more pity than I have ever had in one sitting and leave. I decide to do the same.

On the way back to Santa Marta, the view from the top of the hill is spectacular. Light brown cactus-covered hills sweep into a green and white valley where simple houses, only just this side of shanty, are nestling among small trees and dusty roads. Beyond them, the town sits on its narrow strip, the ship's famous Blue Star funnel towering over the dock and, in the distance, I can just see Isla de la Aguja sitting in a Caribbean that looks like a blue, sequinned, satin cloak flung about the world like the Virgin Mary's mantle.

Compared to El Rodadero, Santa Marta suddenly looks interesting, so I tell the driver I'll walk back. In a rush of Spanish which falls like colourful beads about me and means less, he indicates that it is fine here and on the beach over there but, he points dramatically to the dock gate, it is definitely not fine there and he pulls at his gold chain, and then points at my ringed finger and mimes someone removing both, followed by someone slitting his throat. So I agree to meet him in an hour, and he goes off wreathed in smiles.

In the Parque de Simón Bolívar in the middle of the town, the great liberator is mounted on such a huge horse and base it is quite difficult to see him from the ground. Along the wide, paved avenue, a handful of traders have laid out a few wares on threadbare rugs. Jewellery made from shells and beads and wan-looking, partially disabled plastic dolls do nothing for my need to contribute to their personal economies; all the same, I search eagerly before reminding myself of the chore of dragging home junk that will only ever amount to a growing storage and disposal problem. Never mind the dusting.

I cross the busy road to the beach where I see a stall festooned with shoes and sandals in such beautiful burnished leathers they cry out to be stroked. A young woman with a river of glossy black hair and a money belt gasps an involuntary gasp when I ask, as nonchalantly as possible, whether she has any in *cuarenta y tres*. Assuming I can't count in Spanish, she looks down at my feet and gasps again, looking at me with so much pity I start to cry. She has flung me back to Wellington, age 16, when I had to sleep all night in my new white stilettos, as it was the only way I could foresee hobbling the following night away at the school dance. 'No one makes shoes to fit you, it's those or nothing,' the woman in Wellington had told me in clipped tones, and I can still see her bored look out the window as she spoke. 'Besides, they will stretch.' Then I did not cry. And since then I have met many reactions in shoe outlets, but this is the first time I have met sympathy. As my tears fall, she gently takes my hand and leads me to a three-legged stool where we both perch precariously while she strokes the back of my hand, murmuring 'there-theres' and 'never-minds', clearly thinking me undone by my self-confessed freakishness. Meanwhile, her sister comes and goes, trying to force endless pairs of unprepossessing sandals onto feet growing even larger in the heat. Just because I take *cuarenta y tres* doesn't mean I wear any old thing, I don't attempt to say. They mean so well.

Fortunately, a wizened man crouching on spindly legs is frying kebabs on a primus so near our stool that I am gagging on the smell of kerosene and burning flesh, so I pull myself together and promise to come back soon. Very soon. Fortunately, they don't seem to mind that I don't want their shoes, but are going about saying 'fawtee thrrree,' 'you need fawtee thrrree,' and laughing with delight at being able to practise their Eengleesh, and not appearing to think my little foray into delayed grief at all strange. Emotion is legal here.

At the dock gate, Juan, who is struggling along under a pile of Vision Ware saucepans, tells me that the cook and the messman have been robbed at gunpoint by three men. They lost a ghetto blaster they were taking to play on the beach (super), as well as an expensive camera one of the wipers had lent them, their conspicuously expensive watches and $300.

H is busy all afternoon with men from various ministries who call apparently to inspect things, but really to collect their swag. When he finally appears in the late afternoon, he tells me that the agent is sending a car in half an hour so we can have dinner ashore. Unfortunately, when our transport arrives two hours late, it is the agent's very small pickup and we have to squeeze into the front with the agent and his wife, which means I'm on H's knee with my neck at an excruciating angle. Apparently, the alternative was a motorbike delivering us one at a time. The agent apologises profusely for his lateness and explains that, just as he was leaving, the head banana man turned up, wanting a conference with the head stevedore, and by the time he got that organised, well … what could he do, and he lifts his eyebrows high, and takes his hands off the wheel, which makes me twist a bit more and dig my buttock bones into H's thighs, which still have enough feeling for a wince. Because of my neck position, I can't see his wife, but I know she is sandwiched between H and the agent, because I can see a pair of small feet with red toenails.

At Calle 13, we insist on getting out, but we do have to insist as they appear desperate to take us sightseeing and then over to Rodadero as though we are not in a contorted heap. 'They were only being polite,' I say unfolding myself as the pickup creeps away. H is worrying that we have appeared rude or ungrateful or both. 'They would have hated us if we'd stayed a moment longer. All that desolation is just oiling the social wheels.' While I do believe this, I am still puzzled, as they appeared, when we parted, to be in the early stages of grief.

Calle 13 is Santa Marta's principal shopping street, but the shops are all about to close and in no time we are either staring at shutters or peering into darkened windows trying to make out prices. As the lights go out one by one, the street becomes deserted until, from out of the shadows, a man with a grubby bag stands in our path and pushes a fistful of Ray-Bans and Anaïs Anaïs perfume bottles under our surprised noses saying, 'Try, try, you try,' in a menacing tone. In the gloom, he looks like a skeleton with a few well-spaced, worn-down teeth hanging over bloodless lips. Before we can explain we have no call for either product, we are surrounded by skeletons with plastic bags and, no matter how briskly we walk or how studiously we ignore them, we are soon leading a straggly muttering procession growing in size and menace. It is rather like being followed by excited bullocks who think you have food; any false move and they could go wild and trample you to death.

When the shops disappear, the street narrows and darkens, and we are surrounded by high unscalable walls. Feeling both ridiculous and alarmed, we quicken and lengthen our strides as our pursuers' mutterings fast become hostile. Once or twice, they attempt to grab our clothing and, as we pull away, I suggest to H that we deal with them as we might bullocks, i.e. turn on them suddenly, waving our arms and shouting, 'get on you buggers, get on you buggers'. We are feverishly debating the effectiveness of this when we turn a corner into the spacious square and the motley procession disappears into the shadows again.

To recover, we stop for a while near the statue of Bolívar where a reverential crowd are crouching on their haunches and gazing in rapture at a small woman who is singing, dancing and preaching, sometimes with something near abandon. From time to time, the crowd bursts into wild clapping and whooping while acolytes with beatific grins set out pots of food stopping occasionally to break into ecstatic dancing. Had I dropped in from Mars, I would make no sense of this. But as I haven't, I know that the destitute of Santa Marta are being fed while their souls are canvassed. I have always thought this combination a great pity. If only they would drop the message. The truth can always speak for itself.

It doesn't take long to walk the length of Avenida Rodrigo de Bastidas, the boulevard on the front, where the bars are either dark, thudding caves or brightly-lit glass verandas where motionless men stare like statues at Colombia playing football on television. Leaning in through the wide-open café windows are what look like heaps of stickmen piled up like rags. Suddenly they fly up screaming, screeching and dancing maniacally all over our feet, and spilling like a demented tide into the path of crowded buses. For a few minutes there is mayhem, and then as quickly as it came in, the tide recedes leaving behind only a man in a tee-shirt which reads, 'Every mother is a working mother', who asks in English if we would like a guide. Reluctantly we shake his hand, which feels like a warm and very damp rag overdue for wringing out, trying not to be repulsed by the limp grey plugs of hair straggling over his ears and clinging to his papery cheeks, and his mad unfocussed eyes. 'I can show you many things,' he says dancing along in front of us, trying and failing to look like a needy puppy, and only giving up when the crowds are so thick he can't dance backwards safely. As the night deepens, the crowds on the pavement sway and swing as though they are one body, while other crowds squeeze on and off buses. All of Santa Marta, it seems, is partying.

Thanks to Nicole's map we soon find the Pan Americano and discover it has more than one restaurant, plus a couple of television lounges whose clients are spilling on to the street. We hover for a moment, unsure where we belong. Suddenly, the double glass doors of an inner sanctum swing open, and a suave man in nautical uniform (three stripes) glides on rollers towards us saying, 'Theese way pleeze,' with great authority. We follow obediently into a room where the tables are dressed to the floor in multi-layered, pink damask and every other surface is muted and hushed by drapes, carpets and assorted hangings. It's almost as though we, the real spenders, must be guaranteed a refined hush to separate us from the unconfined clamour in the streets and the deafening mayhem in the football lounges whenever Colombia scores. The doors swish shut behind us and we are handed menus the size of a novel and bowed to. And Nicole is right—it's freezing.

I am well overdue food and beginning to get tetchy, and I am certainly not in the mood to wade through a huge menu in a room decorated as though it were a ship. From the ceiling hang acres of ruched white sails, and marching around the walls are small, painted, stained-glass portholes depicting yachts, desert islands and birds gliding above garishly blue rolling waves. At the end of the room, three large arched windows are painted with fish, buried treasure and the odd pirate with one eye and a telescope. This separates us from the football lounge, which we can no longer hear; in fact, it is so quiet we can hear ourselves breathing.

When we get our fruits of the season (H) and mixed fish in vinaigrette starters, there is only one other table occupied by a couple who are in the grip of uncontrollable passion, to judge by the fervid and blatant doings under the damask. But H is too busy avoiding the tiny flies which are hatching from his melon to be interested. 'We'll have to get a phrasebook,' he says. 'One that tells us how to say, "Flies are hatching from my melon".'

'They probably haven't got anywhere else to do it,' I suggest, referring to the couple, although naturally H assumes I mean the flies.

During our main course, a large, well-turned-out, handsome family resembling the cast of a continental art film, move into several tables pushed together, very near our elbows. A forty-something man constantly waves his arm dangerously near H's head, summoning the waiters. If not attended to immediately, he swivels erratically or claws the air impatiently with maddened fingers, as though scratching an invisible itch. When the gliding waiters bring whatever he demands—which they do so quickly our shrunken gestures don't get a look in—he extravagantly indicates who is to receive what and then smiles at the grateful person, as though he has personally bought, prepared, cooked, dished and delivered it. In between, there are such lively exchanges with his wife and another couple, we are all lost in a maelstrom of words and gestures.

At the other end of the table, two very small girls are yawning, shivering and far too tired to eat. Perhaps they are five, certainly no more, and every rich shining brown hair has been braided into the tiniest bejewelled ringlets. Their thin angular bodies are in flimsy multi-frilled dresses that expose frozen shoulders and long thin limbs. But no one notices. A teenage boy occasionally talks to them, and a handsome grandmother smiles slightly sadly; otherwise they are ignored. Eventually one flops forward into her food, asleep. The other bends her legs under her chin and struggles to pull the damask around her frozen little body. I can hardly control my need to warm them up. But I do.

When we ask for the bill, we are told in perfect English that the tip is not included. These are the only words of English we have heard all night. What's more, his tone is a reprimand. We tip generously and don't mention the flies.

Outside, music is thumping out of every café and the streets are thick with revelry. We cross to the tranquillity of the beach and find the darkened sands alive with plastic bag desperadoes, who come after us with their, 'You want Rolex' and their pushing, shoving and grabbing routines. Without a word, we head for the busy bright market stalls and, as we are about to flop into the nearest taxi, we hear, 'Fawtee thrree, you want fawtee thrree' and there she is, with her sister smiling and waving, as though we are firm friends. In no time, a small crowd is peering in at us, just in case we are celebrities, minor or major. 'Puerto Marítimo, gracias,' I say to a driver who looks very pleased to be dealing with people of consequence.

Back at the ship, we find the head of the banana company and the foreman in conference on the orderly but frenetic dock. We pick our way through trucks and under conveyor belts surrounded by men, mess and noise so H can ask when we will be sailing. 'We are hoping to be finishing tomorrow, early,' says the foreman, and the banana king asks how I like Santa Marta.

'Very much,' I say, with masses of enthusiasm which I feel, 'But next time I'd like to see the house where Simón Bolívar died, and the museum,' I add, knowing that it contains a scale model of Cuidad Perdida, the largest pre-Colombian town in the Americas, as well as lots of other relics and artefacts of the region.

They both look surprised. 'This is a very dangeruse place where Simón Bolívar house is. You should not go there alone. Very dangeruse. You should not go there.' The words roll out like huge ominous boulders. He looks hard to see if they have squashed me and that I have grasped his meaning, which I have. I smile winningly. He softens. I am forgiven. 'Never mind. Next time I will take you and show you everything,' and he waves his large arms to the max, meaning that next time no sightseeing stone will be left unturned. For us, Santa Marta will be laid bare. I add a pinch of gratitude to my smile.

'Thank you,' says H. 'That would be very nice,' and we negotiate the rest of the obstacle-strewn dock, safe in the knowledge that next time he will have no memory of his grand generosity. In fact, next time he will have no idea who we are.

37 Stacking the boxes

38 Steering the pallets

HEADING HOME

As the *Chiquita Scandinavia* is berthing just before breakfast, a gang in neat brown overalls and hard hats are cleaning the dock. Their supervisor, in lemon overalls, is making sure no sliver of cardboard or file of binding escapes. It's more performance art than cleaning, especially when the pigeons suddenly swoosh into the sky, swifts dart about gobbling insects, and the joint haloes on the hill glint like stage lights.

'The police raided the disco last night Ma'am,' Juan tells me on about my third spoonful of cereal. In every port the Filipinos' disco detecting devices seek out the hottest places which then become the measure of a port's worth. Just as turning to bleary-eyed and scratching is a measure of how good the night has been. But Juan looks fresh enough. 'They frisked everyone and then went away,' he adds when he comes back with my toast and coffee.

H phones to say that Nina, the new provedore, is down to introduce herself and would like to meet me, which means she wants to use me to soften H's buying heart. I find them in the conference room having a working coffee, and can't resist saying, 'What's happened to Nicole?'

'Nicole has gun,' she says.

'Gone?'

'Gun,' she repeats.

'Is she all right? Will she be coming back?'

'No, she won't be coming. She is fine, I think (this is a little airy). But I am the provedore now,' and she turns a high beam on H from exceptionally bright eyes. H looks uncomfortable, as though she might be about to suggest lap dancing. He says something about needing to sort out the labour and eases his way out, apologising to Nina. She swings around to face me, barely disturbing the impeccable cut of her linen trousers and silk shirt, and says, in a tone dripping in understanding, 'He's a busy man.' Instead of going completely floppy and/or snorting, I forgive her this piece of nonsense, not because it isn't true but because he could be the most indolent slob on the planet and she would still say it. And of course it is a mind-numbing mantra, one of many which dog me on the trail, 'going ashore to spend all his money' easily being the worst as it is wheeled out every time we are in port. 'Do you like Santa Marta?' Nina chirrups.

'It's beautiful, especially from the sea and so different from Turbo. Is it always so orderly and … um peaceful?'

'Peaceful? Yes, mostly. But sometimes, there is trouble with the guerrillas if they come down from the mountains.'

I am surprised at this mention of guerrillas so soon. 'Does that happen often?' I am also terribly interested, but try not to sound it.

'Not so often at this time, but very many stay in the Sierras very near to Santa Marta and sometimes they come down and there is beeg trouble.'

'Who are they?'

'They are the terrorists and communists, and they want to overthrow the government,' she says sounding rather like the Queen Mother describing old Labour, and from which I assume they are the FARC (Revolutionary Armed forces of Colombia). 'But it is worse in Turbo. There is always trouble. It is never safe from the guerrillas.' Nina is either not keen on talking specifics or, more likely, not that clear about who they are and what they do. The Colombian guerrilla has many faces and causes, ranging from those who would consider themselves peaceful, e.g. Catholic priests offering social services where none exist, to extreme right-wing paramilitary groups intent on getting rid of 'turbulent priests' and their flocks and not that bothered how they do it. 'Never mind. It is better here. And next time you come, I will show you everything. First in Santa Marta and then we will go to Rodadero. Have you been in Rodadero?'

'Yes,' I say, 'but I haven't seen Simón Bolívar's house yet.'

Nina's beams fade. 'The house of Simón Bolívar is in a dangerous place,' and she frowns and looks genuinely puzzled, as though she has never heard of anyone being interested in Simón, let alone his house. She's thinking I have ideas above my station and changes tack. 'Next time you are here,' she is beaming again, 'what say I take you to Cartagena and Barranquilla? I have a very good idea, why don't you stay in Santa Marta and enjoy yourself while your husband works, and we could have four or five days together and then you could join him in Turbo?' This is an extraordinary offer from someone I've only just met, so I assume she is so desperate to make a sale that she is prepared to do anything, or at least suggest it. H is possibly her first job and, like Nicole, she could be 'gun' next time if the authorities suspect her of boarding before the ship is cleared. 'When will you be back? Send a telex when you will be back, and we can have a good time together for many days while the captain works. Do you like shopping?' I knew we wouldn't get far without the S word, but I know this is all just chat and part of her job, so say, 'That would be great, thanks very much,' safe in the knowledge that she will not be holding her breath for that telex and that tomorrow, or later today, she will be saying the same thing to some other partner and—who knows—we could all end up exploring Colombia with Nina, just so she can get a measly order for a few fags and some whisky.

'The loading is finished, but we are waiting for one truck,' H says when he reappears and Nina has beamed out. 'The pilot is pacing about on the bridge, getting more and more agitated and threatening to leave.'

Just then, two limos purr onto the otherwise deserted dock, and several men in black lumber out and start to conference. Apart from their wraparound shades, they are dressed for a funeral. From time to time, they talk into phones as though they are eating them, or they swagger over and consult mountainous-looking minders waiting at an indiscreet distance. Gripped by this performance, I snap their antics from our deck, ducking into the light and back into the shadows in the time it takes to say 'smile'. Unfortunately, one of the heavies spots me and points, and they all turn and look up. With a pounding heart, I rush inside and lock the door, waiting for the stairwell to fill with thudding footsteps and raised voices. I visualise the door being kicked in and the camera and self being wasted. (It's the heat.)

When H enquires about the delay, he is told by the boss himself, and rather inexplicably, that the price of bananas is good in Europe. H suggests calmly and logically that waiting for one truck is not really on because for every hour lost, we will have to go faster and burn a small fortune in heavy fuel. Even waiting for twenty trucks for one hour would be silly. His maths degree is showing.

'You told a man in wraparound shades with mountainous minders that he was silly—to his face?' I say, feeling my love ratcheting up yet again. H is morally brave; nothing impresses him more than straightness. Being straight was one of the phrases I remember plopping into our conversations early on, when I might have overlooked a bit of moral compromising. That and 'it wouldn't be proper'. I instantly liked the fact that 'proper' was not the language of the Sixties generation, who believed they redefined propriety. So, despite several social movements washing over society, when their tides ran out, there was H still in his moral landscape with the signposts still reading 'straight' and 'proper'. And so I discovered that he is never afraid to speak his mind, regardless of the supposed weight of his audience. Underdogs in his care benefit from this moral courage. And such things are very important in a marriage. But equally important is our liking early nights, sitting with our feet up, and eating at the same time. Happy unions are built on everydayness.

'I said it because it's true. That truck could be anywhere, and it is extremely fishy to up the fuel bill by far more than one truckload of bananas could ever make. And if we run into bad weather and have to slow down, I don't want to feel pushed to keep the speed up.' Of course, like the rest of us, H just wants to go. But what he wants is as irrelevant as what I want. He's the driver, whether and when we go is not for him to decide. Someone on land decides all that.

While we are hanging about, the *Winter Sea* comes alongside and a flotilla of colourfully decorated trucks gathers about it. Some drivers sling hammocks in the shade of their wheelbases and are soon sleeping, while others roll back the canvas tops, or lift off the white lattice sides so small yellow forklift trucks can scurry back and forward like ants, offloading the boxes and depositing them near the ship's cranes.

As the delay drags on, the conferencing on the dock seems to stalemate. The pilot, fed up with pacing about the bridge, runs down the gangway in a huff. The guard on the dock changes—two fresh-faced angels present arms to two extremely sleepy ones who have been there all night. The crew get restive; their mouths are watering at the thought of barbecuing the great marlin the bosun brought back from Taganga, a fishing village in the next bay. It's just the start of some serious New Year feasting and the mere thought they may have to delay their gratification does not please them.

Eventually, though there is still no sign of the missing truck, the limos purr off into the heat haze, and we are told to sail. Immensely relieved, the pilot appears from nowhere and skips up the gangway and the *Barranquilla* tugs us away stern first. It's 13.25, the aquamarine sea is ruffled by a slight breeze, and all about us are clouds of multi-coloured butterflies. Above the shimmering town, the slowly-shrinking hills look baked hard, every peak sharp, every ridge like a crust. As we pass the Morro Grande, the pilot calls 'dead slow ahead,' then 'stop engines,' and as he leaves the bridge he bows to me, saying, 'Have a happy journey. I'll see you next time.'

By evening, the smell of barbecued fish has slipped into every duct and passageway. At seven, we listen to the morose tolling of Big Ben on the World Service, marking midnight in Scotland, then join the rest on deck where the karaoke is wailing, and a violent wind is doing its best to rip our clothes off and send what's left of the food flying. Eventually we all give up, and anyone with excess energy carries on in the crew bar, which means we can retire gracefully and observe Hogmanay horizontally.

Our carefree sailing days are over and it's full speed ahead to drop the first lot of greens in Marin on the Atlantic coast of Spain. From now on, H will be both cargo- (condition of) and speed-obsessed. His calculator at the ready, he will constantly be working out what speed we need to reach our ETA taking into account incalculables like weather, wave size and what say we have to stop for repairs. We will always be going too fast or too slow, and H will be saying to the other officers, 'How's the speed?' many times a day.

That's the downside; the upside is that we are now down by the head and stern and far less likely to fly out of the water and slam down again in an unpleasant way, so my breakfast may be safe in my stomach, and we will all sleep better.

After morning smoko, H relieves the third officer on the bridge so he can check the temperatures in the hatches, known as 'doing the pulps.' Bananas are carried at 13.3 degrees Celsius; they are a delicate cargo and even a tenth of a degree can make a difference. Too high and they start producing ethylene gas, a natural hormone which ripens them; too low and they blacken and freeze. Fortunately, any average nose can sniff out premature ripening, but 'I smelt ripes, Sir,' is not a phrase any banana-carrying captain likes to hear, as one yellow can ripen a cargo quite quickly. The third officer likes doing the pulps; it is a cold job, but it's not arduous or dangerous, despite the slight chance he could poke his temperature probe into a stowaway's flesh. Slight, because they usually hide, well surrounded by boxes and can't move far. Until recently, though, the loaded hatches were not locked and, if they stowed away near the exit, they could get out at night to warm up, stretch their cramped legs and steal food from the lifeboats and the galley. I am yet to meet a stowaway in the galley at night, but on less secure ships it's not uncommon these days, with so many taking this travel option.

The highlight of New Year's Day for the Filipinos—after they have roasted yet another pig on deck—is the horse race. Whether on land or at sea, I have never been other than mildly bored by racing of any kind (whippet, frog or human), and much as I love horses, their sinewy bodies and silken manes are not enhanced when mounted by small men with whips. However, substitute brightly-painted wooden horses with no legs for the real thing, and my mild boredom becomes indifference. To the Filipinos, however, horseracing is the nearest they get to nirvana, especially after so much feasting. Their excitement bubbles away for days before, and after, they talk of little else.

When, after lunch, I finally persuade myself to swap the silence of the suite for the din in the officers' lounge, a queue is already snaking towards the tote (H and the chief at a makeshift table), and an AB is bawling, 'Place your bets ladies and gentleman, place your bets for race one now,' into the karaoke mic and singing, 'Why, why, why, Delilah,' with a painful vibrato between announcements. Behind the bar, the CD is wailing something else at full volume, and the television is playing a maudlin karaoke tape. It's more madhouse than Epsom, with everyone milling about in their best casuals, smiling stupidly and making sure they don't walk on the course which H has drawn on the back of several old charts and spread out on the deck. He has also produced a programme.

There are five races, some flat, some with hurdles (miss a turn/start again), and we each move our horse (or not) after throwing two large dice. When the odds are up on the board and race one starts, we all sit sedately with arms folded or lean forward, showing polite interest. When someone throws a six, we whoop; when the huge red dice rolls with the ship the length of the lounge, we laugh. And when the deck fitter crosses the line miles ahead of the field we cheer. Between races, the commentator again competes with the CD player and the television while we collect winnings, rip tabs off cans, light fags and choose our bets for race two.

Again, it starts quietly. But this time there are handicaps and when the leader by miles has to go back to the beginning, the mood changes and a few anxious punters get up and bawl a bit. Then a few more join in and slowly the noise level rises until, like a fire suddenly finding oxygen, the room is full of an unholy racket. Everyone is jostling for a place near the course and cheering, booing, clutching their throats or tearing their hair out while on the paper track the horses lurch about at the mercy of the dice. 'Six, six, six,' or 'one, one, one,' they chant, as the careless dice disappears under chairs and between legs.

39 The horse race

When the second engineer and the engine fitter are at the finishing post, needing only a two to cross, the noise becomes pentecostal. Someone falls to his knees stroking the turf, a few bless themselves, while the rest pray, promise complete reformation, kiss the dice or mutter in tongues. But it is all useless. Neither horse manages to cross, and the rest of the field are on their tails, threatening to snatch victory.

Then the second engineer does it. We stare for a silent second as though unable to register the fact, and then the noise goes off the scale. Wild cheers whoop off every bulkhead, bodies cling together in dancing heaps, or leap about like demented goats, their eyes on the winner. The hero. The Olympian. As befits one suddenly great, an unhinged second engineer struts about the room, legs as stiff as his horse, alternately raising his eyes to heaven and kissing anyone he walks into. Finally, wound up to the max, he strides right out the door and back through the saloon as though in perpetual motion.

I should mention that winning is not just about the money; the glory catapults you to another world. And of course you have won a place in the final and the chance of even more money and glory.

40 Running the tote

Slowly we all breathe out, sitting again to slow our pulses, slinking off to lick wounds, or queuing to collect winnings. And so it goes on for an entire afternoon and evening: race after ridiculous race, running the gamut between heart-stopping suspense and abject disappointment. And I endure this emotional merry-go-round by coming and going so that I am not continuously inhaling fatal doses of second hand smoke. But when my horse—Fish out of Water—wins the Donkey Derby and so loses the race and a wad of dollars, I go out on deck, as the tubercular once went to Switzerland, and gulp until my tight chest lets go a bit and I can no longer smell and taste tar. To my astonishment, I see that we are in Mona Passage, which is the route we are taking between the Caribbean and the Atlantic. This is all the excuse I need to give the races a miss. At least for a while.

The way we come and go from the Caribbean is H's decision, based on time of year, likelihood of hurricanes (worse than stowaways but this is not the season), destination ports and weather forecasts. Once the passage has been selected, the second officer marks the charts in pencil, and afterwards rubs it all out. Odd to see in this computer age, but not on ships this age. When the charts are passage ready, H checks that the second officer hasn't drawn lines over rocks and through submerged obstacles, which does happen, and not always because there are many uncharted rocks.

In choosing the passage, H can consult Ocean Routes, a weather forecasting company, who either confirm his choice or suggest another, based on their specialist knowledge of what storms or swells are in the offing days hence. The charterer pays, concerned that the bananas have the best possible chance of arriving on time, and H uses it even though they have at times sent him into the teeth of gales or mountainous swells.

Mona Passage lies between the Dominican Republic and Puerto Rico and is not difficult to navigate; even at its narrowest, it is 61 miles wide and there are no tricky changes of course.

What makes Mona an event, apart from the superb visibility and lovely weather, is three islands: Mona, Monito and Desecheo. As I lean on the rail, the sea at its most benign and inviting, Isla de Mona is just beginning to draw a line on the horizon. Nearer, it becomes a rising pancake; then, at nine miles, the closest we get, it is like a neat, elongated cake, smooth and flat with steep, straight sides. According to the pilot book, the flat top is covered in cactus and the uniform sides full of caves, but to me it is bald and bare, and as it grows smaller with the sun bouncing off its smooth chalky sides, it becomes a milky greenstone—jade perhaps—set in a blue-gold sea.

At 20 knots, it is not long before Isla Monito pokes its punkish head over Mona's flat top and quickly grows into a high, bare, steep and jagged rock. Far away to starboard and washed with haze, Puerto Rico rises and dips about the horizon, and from time to time flocks of frigate birds scrawl darkened spirals in the blue above the bridge, while one breaks away and swoops about the bow. It's a wonderful show, but I have responsibilities elsewhere!

Back at the races, anyone not collecting winnings or queuing to bet on race five—the Santa Marta Gold Cup—is writhing to Romeo's Bee Gees' imitation. Around the dancers, thin trails of smoke are winding gracefully like sinister streamers. Through the double doors, the stewards are swinging in and out of the saloon with large platters, glasses and cutlery.

At the end of race six—the Turbo Classic—H announces the buffet, a lavish spread of salads, chicken, pasta, rice and spring rolls and a trough of mangoes, pineapples and pawpaw. Spirits are high; even the losers are smiling. Perhaps if they'd had horseracing on the *Bounty*, a lot of Tahitians would never have been transplanted to fortress Pitcairn.

It's a relief to see fresh tropical fruit salad. The Filipinos would rather open tins, especially for a fiesta, not because they prefer the tasteless, flaccid fruit but because they believe we do. 'Fruit in tin' appearing on the menu is bad enough anywhere, but in the tropics, where the real exotic thing is piled up in our cold room, it is worse than swede in tin would be in Scotland, although not as bad as 'evaporated milk in rusty tin'. We never have fresh cream at sea these days, although occasionally cream appears on the menu as an accompaniment to 'fruit in tin', and I always fall for it, forgetting that a tin of evaporated milk, which may or may not be rusty, with two blunt holes jabbed in the top, will appear wrapped in a paper napkin, as though it were wine. But to the Filipinos, tinned things are exotic. Which is not surprising. They put pineapples in tins for us for decades. And where we go they follow. At the moment.

When the six winners eventually line up for the final, the lounge is part smoky bar, part Ladbrokes on a Saturday afternoon. Betting is heavy, big losers look desperate, big winners swagger and the rest are mildly hysterical or euphoric. 'They're away, ladies and gentlemen,' booms the commentator when the first dice is thrown, and again it is as though someone has flicked a switch or ordered everyone to screech, curse, bawl, pray and chant, until even the engine can't be heard. Then suddenly it stops. The bosun's horse has flown across the finishing line miles ahead of the rest of the field, taking everyone completely by surprise and resulting in a full-blown anti-climax. Morale is briefly restored when H reminds them they still have lots of place money to play for. But they are not interested; the chance for glory has gone. Being placed does not matter. And when he tries to make a ceremony of the prize-giving, refusing to pay the betting money until due formalities are done, they are mystified. A cultural divide has opened which he is not bridging.

But there's still the dancing to restore fiesta mode so, as one or two disastrous losers slink away too deep in the slough of despond to celebrate, the winners grab Ernesto, the messman, stick a guitar in his hand and order songs as they normally order food. Ernesto is a class act and can play anything in any key and is far too talented to be running after people all day for a pittance and ironing his evenings away for a bit extra. Which is what he does on here.

On the balmy deck under the stars my chest feeling as though it is full of gravel, we watch the lights of Puerto Rico rising and dipping on the horizon. Unfortunately it's too dark to see Desecheo. Later, flat out on the settee we listen to Emanuel Ax with André Previn playing Mozart's Fifth Piano Concerto in a live relay from San Francisco. By the second movement, I can breathe again and it is almost as though the whole demented horserace has never happened.

THE ATLANTIC (AGAIN)

We are in the Atlantic again, about fifty miles north of Puerto Rico, and H has had a telex from the offshore management company asking if there is anyone on board, perhaps a wife, who would be willing to run up a few curtains. This is their whacky response to H's suggestion that they replace the salt-encrusted rags in the officer's lounge (for starters). As they know I am the only wife, it seems a strange way to offer me a job. There could be a bonus in it, they add as an afterthought, in case the wife of the captain objects to being a novel source of cheap labour.

I should explain here the complicated way ships are run these days and how the master has to juggle not just the owner's—but many other—interests. Of course, his first job is to represent the owner, although the irony is that these days he is unlikely ever to have met the owner, not because the owner is too busy or not interested, but because managers of foreign-flagged ships prefer to keep owners and masters apart. Before flagging-out he met the owners quite regularly, but these days whatever owners know about the running of their ships, they don't get it from masters, because the shore staff believe they may know how to navigate but have no place in company politics.

The *Avelona Star* is owned by the Vestey family and H, the chief engineer and the chief officer are employed by a British management company, which is owned and run by the Vesteys. This ship is part of their reefer fleet (refrigerated ships) which they run in conjunction with a

German company. Most of these reefers are not British-manned at all, but this one has British senior officers at the owners' specific request.

The rest of the officers and ratings are managed by the offshore management company (who sent the curtain telex) and they in turn get the Filipinos from one of the many agencies in Manila. One of the two better ones it is said. This offshore management company also runs the ship, which means the owner pays it to be responsible for all repairs, furnishing etc. Naturally, these offshore managers also want to make a profit, so they try to spend as little as possible and are not that concerned how the sea staff live. (It seems.)

The cargo is the concern of the owners' reefer company and the charterer who have chartered the ship for a number of years or a number of voyages.

All this managerial complication is relatively new and the result of modern communications allowing more and more power to be devolved to the land. It is not so long ago that masters had phenomenal power. Once the ship had left port, the office staff could do nothing but bite their nails and wait. Now with satellites tracking everything that moves on land and sea, all decisions are taken ashore, often by people who may never even have been on a ship. They may also have rudimentary people-managing skills or be inclined to regard sea staff as a necessary encumbrance. The result is that when a master makes decisions which would once have been his alone, e.g. whether to use a pilot or not, the merest clerk will feel no compunction about upbraiding him for the expense, having no idea of what is involved. H was once taken to task for ordering a Baltic pilot going into Saint Petersburg, despite it being recommended. He had been up for 30 hours in fog all the way up the English Channel, and was due in Vlissingen in Holland in the early morning. After a day's work on no sleep, he had to sail the ship into the North Sea with no idea what conditions may keep him up for another 30 hours. This, as you now know, is not uncommon. The office clerk decided H didn't need a pilot, based on coloured markers he was moving about a board. H made his decision on safety grounds; both his health and the ship's safety could have been in danger. Coloured markers do not sleep and do not feel stress.

I maintain a dignified and very amused silence about the curtains. It is probably the solitary brainwave of a one-idea clodhopper anxious to make his mark. But naturally this makes us all remember the not very distant days when the owner's wife chose the curtains. Days when the windows, with their highly-polished brass window fittings, were draped in the best, always with double linings and a Made in Liverpool embroidered label. Nowadays, if the master wants his ship looking decent, and there are no passengers to spur the management into it, he is advised to find cheap labour in the cheapest foreign port, and take what he can get from a selection of garish fabrics, which are neither pre-shrunk nor colourfast, and which seldom hang right after the first wash. Or before. You can forget double linings that keep the light out for officers having to sleep at all hours of the day. What are airline shades for?

Most masters have little curtain experience; it was not part of their tickets. So, why not give a wife something to do. In accountancy terms, we are a perk. If banning us is not an option, then suggesting we run up curtains obviously is, and the next step could be cooking, laundry and scrubbing floors.

Of course there's a veritable mountain of 'stuff' around women at sea, a great deal of it self-interested superstition and as old as sailing. It makes life hard for women who want to work at sea, of which there are a growing number and, for those of us indulgently trailing, there are plenty of 'hilarious' reminders.

Travelling wives were introduced sometime in the Sixties, not because social consciences were hurting and enlightened managements wanted to make real political rhetoric about the sacredness of the family. Like most other enlightened policies, it was the result of not being able to get people. Men did not want to go to sea for anything up to two years, sometimes longer, without some hope of being able to travel with their families. There have never been hordes of takers—child-rearing and careers see to that—so it has not been a huge expense, particularly in the beginning, when most ships came and went from Britain and long haul airfares were unknown.

Yet the policy has kept many senior officers at sea, especially since downsizing and flagging-out made loneliness and overwork the norm. Not everyone can take months of rattling about on a large ship responsible for everything and with only one, or sometimes two other British officers to talk to, officers you may have nothing in common with—indeed may wish gone. It's not surprising that for want of social support, some lose the place and pack up, or that others pack it in before that happens. They were never trained as monks. In this climate, a partner is a very cheap solution to a huge problem.

H decides to offer the sewing bonus to the catering staff and when Juan hears about the possibility of making curtains, he is very excited even though he cannot sew and has never used a machine. 'Romeo will show me,' he says at lunchtime. 'He is a trained tailor and will show me everything, Sir.' Is there no end to the strings on Romeo's bow? Juan is certainly keen to add a few more strings to his bow and is excited at the thought of the bonus. I can already hear him in the agency in Manila saying, 'Upholstery? No problem, I refurbished my last ship, Sir.'

Juan is already extremely proud of his catering skills, but not ready to rest on his laurels. As I am munching on the apple he presents on a plate with a knife and napkin, he says, 'I have my training manual Ma'am, if you would like to see it,' and before I can say 'Mrs Beaton', I am reading a copperplate-filled exercise book (I am yet to meet the Filipino who did not have beautiful handwriting which he had clearly spent hours perfecting) full of riveting housekeeping advice from the era when women with wasp waists, Toni perms and perfect makeup went about behind vacuum cleaners in their best clothes and pinnies (frilled)—in the male fantasy ads anyway. Like dinosaurs, these women and their manuals have died out; unlike dinosaurs, we always knew why.

All the same, Juan's book is interesting, if slightly less so than a book about dinosaurs. It's also hectoring and bossy as wifely manuals always were: 'Always use a separate knife and board for chopping onions and garlic,' and 'make sure he has a balanced diet … show him you care'. It's the tone; as though they are addressing halfwits, which of course they assumed they were. I flip through advice on how to iron, starch, clean windows without smearing, and turn to the hard information about foods and their components and values. It's good stuff and readable enough, as a popular scientific book is readable. But finding the big bang theory interesting does not mean I want to do the experiments.

When I hand it back, Juan hovers. Then I realise that this is curtain-related. He wants me to recommend him. From my unique standpoint as one of nature's eager curtain-makers, I am to pronounce him a potential furnisher. I give the nod and H, looking a bit mystified by the catering politics, says he will let him have the machine to practise on until the material comes in Belgium. 'If you give me a quote for the job, I'll telex and find out what the bonus is exactly.' H doesn't like words like 'there could be' in business arrangements. It's neither straight nor proper.

'A quote, Sir. Yes, I will do that,' and his eyes shine as he pours us more water.

And so we all save face. It will not be on the galley radio that the poor captain is saddled with someone who can't or, worse, won't sew. I can sew of course, but life is short and I have always known about priorities and from an early age have had them. But when push has come to shove, I have proved myself more than adequate at the Singer.

I no longer sew, just as it is several decades since I have ironed. When I was flatting, and long before feminism backed me up, I charged men to iron their shirts, knowing they don't like to pay when the next man is getting it free. I watched as my flatmates spent the best years of their lives pinioned to ironing boards while their partners lounged about watching television. In our house now, neither of us irons, having discovered it was unnecessary. We believe we still own an iron, but it is some time since we knew where it was.

It's fire and boat drill again so, later in the day, we all crowd round the pool to watch Romeo fall in with his lifejacket on to demonstrate that, no matter how you fall into the water, you will end up on your back. It doesn't work, even after several goes. The chief officer and the bosun try, but they, too, drown—or are about to—when they turn themselves over manually, which I hope I will be in a fit state to do. Ideally on a day like today.

It is an exquisite afternoon, so no hardship to stand around the pool. The sun is not only bearable, but it feels as though it is stroking my skin and the golden blue flawless sky is making me want to fly. It seems odd not to be able to fly and swim, surrounded by so much water and sky. I am often severely tempted by the gently rocking, harmless-looking sea and have to remind myself that seductive though it looks, it would definitely be my last dive. Finally, the chief officer comes out of the pool looking puzzled and saying he'll look into the lifejacket failure, and we all shrug and wander off in dribs and drabs, out of the expanding lightness into the constricting depths of the crew bar. It's time for another safety film and this one turns out to be a period piece from the pinny years, i.e. a cautionary tale.

It goes like this: Harry is nice but careless. And not clean. When he catches his sleeve in a shredder and is partially shredded, he ends up flat out on the factory floor, and Betty from the office, who has done a first-aid course, gives him mouth to mouth. And when Harry comes round in hospital, instead of a good talking to about personal hygiene, the nurses are saying, 'poor Harry' and, 'Shame! Such a nice bloke!' as they patch him up.

Naturally, he does it again. And the next thing he's flat on his back, buried in pipes. Betty, still miraculously walking about, resuscitates him again, this time using the Holger Nielsen method for those on their stomachs who can't be moved. As there is no mouth to mouth this is easier to watch. And Betty is good. The crew pass around peanuts and munch loudly, often with their mouths open, as though they are in a cinema and Harry is from Mars. They would certainly not relate to his personal hygiene problem.

Back in our quarters, H and self spend the evening with our ears pressed against bulkheads and staring at cupboards, trying to find the cause of a horrible clunking which has been annoying us all day. When we are in the dayroom, it comes from the bedroom; when we rush in there, it comes from the dayroom or the bathroom and so on. The engine, the cooling fans and the air conditioning I can just about sleep through, with earplugs, because I know what they are and what to expect. But an unidentified, intermittent clunking ...

MORE BAD WEATHER

Noises off at sea can leave us wrecked and likely to descend into irrationality. Last night, as well as the unidentified clunking, the turbo blowers screeched like banshees for hours. How can I describe this provoking din to those who know only crowing cocks, lowing cows or even city sirens, and a procession of 747s? As a graduate of all those, I can safely say that, even all together, they are as music compared to intermittent turbo blowers which stop just long enough for you to drop off before beginning again their random and merciless keening.

Reefer ships are bad for noises, especially old ones. As we tossed and muttered in the early hours, and I went over the 'things I do for you' script, the general cacophony tipped H into action, and he phoned the bridge and ordered the watchman to 'thoroughly investigate that clunking now.' These tiresome conditions are slowly changing H from a totally equable, droll person, to the owner of a wick whose end is in sight. This is more than slightly alarming because (a) his blood pressure and general health will suffer and he may not live to enjoy his pension (which is the *only* reason we are both here) and (b) as well as his supermarket arms, which make him able to carry mountains of carrier bags, I was magnetically attracted to his equanimity.

Of course, there was nothing anyone could do about the turbo blowers without stopping the ship and cleaning them, but the horrible clunking stopped because it was not a rogue screw in the bulkhead but a banging watertight door on the main deck. Apparently, the engineers had been going in and out and either not shutting it (correct procedure) or clipping it back. It's a mystery how the rating who sleeps beside it was staying sane, and why he didn't do something. But I'm told that Filipinos are not bothered by noises off. There could be someone beating a drum by their heads and they would still sleep. Is that a gift from the gods or genetic or stupid or what? And why are we wound up like coils and victims of the merest squeak?

This morning at breakfast, I bit into a semi-rigid fingernail; the emergency Costa Rican bread is sweet and white and far too close to polystyrene even without fingernails. I discovered it while the chief was telling me about the five saddest stowaways ever who came on board from a zungo in Turbo and hid in the locked fo'c'sle, after one of them—a small one—climbed through a pipe under the windlass and let them all in. I'd rather not know about penetrable pipes and what desperadoes will do to sail on here, yet once again I find myself feeling sorry for men with so little to lose. Surely outside of dysfunctional thrill seekers and/or those with a testosterone overload, no one would choose to creep onto a banana boat, unless they are so deeply buried under the social heap it seems the only way up. I certainly do not believe we are born bad or with original sin, whatever that tatty phrase means, but there is evidence that some may have badness thrust upon them, although none whatsoever that crime springs from poverty. This lot, the chief says, were young, possibly feckless and obviously opportunistic, and they were certainly far from typical.

Normally, stowaways for the USA—the ship was going to Florida—are well-organised with papers, money, weapons, drugs and food, and they bribe their way on board. These pitiful beings had only a few crusts of bread and a few bits of clothing, and they boarded at night when everyone, including the guards, was crowded round a radio listening to Colombia v Paraguay at football, an event more absorbing than sex and more sacred than High Mass.

Naturally, because they were in the paint locker, they were discovered the first time someone needed paint. Finding one is bad enough, but five can take over a ship. Fortunately, it was possible to contain these in the locker all the way to the United States and back to Panama, and food, water, and waste matter were exchanged through a slit in the door. It was unbearably hot, the smell was foul, and they had to be guarded day and night, especially in the United States, where there is a heavy fine for ships whose illegals escape. It was a hideous experience for everyone and so bad for the stowaways that they vowed never to do it again. They had all done it before.

The relief telexes have come, which is always news and always exciting for those being relieved. The chief officer, the fourth engineer and three others are getting off in Zeebrugge. I've decided to stand by my man; this is only trip one of four and the scars from the early days have faded. And winter in Scotland isn't unalloyed fun.

The fourth engineer is particularly excited, as he has been here for a year and is so pale he is starting to look yellow. He started his tour as an oiler and three months ago, on the chief's recommendation, he was promoted. The leap from oiler (engine room skivvy) to engineering officer (engine room skivvy with one stripe who can give orders and eat in the officers' dining room) is huge and, although it almost always means an extension of the nine-month contract, most are keen, as it means they are on the way up to chief engineer, a pinnacle from which they can gaze down into the social abyss at sea and at home.

The Filipinos have a strange career structure, strange to us but not in their social context. Whatever their ambition, when they first walk into a recruitment office in Manila, they start at the very bottom as messmen (the closest they can get to being a woman without an operation). This means that, no matter what their qualifications, and some have degrees, when they have done enough cleaning, fetching and carrying, and being ordered about for no status and low pay, they may be lucky and graduate to oiling or wiping engines.

When I asked the newly-promoted fourth engineer at the horserace what he liked best about going home, he said, with rheumy eyes, 'Seeing my dog, Ma'am. She's a stray, and she goes everywhere with me.' This picture of the fourth engineer (who has a sad but lovely face and walks like Charlie Chaplin) with a stray at his heel, did threaten to operate my tear glands. And, I thought later, there'd be no awkward period between them either. No feeling of invasion. The slavish devotion would start from first sight and smell, if I know dogs. Cats can be more standoffish after a period of desertion.

And so can I. When H comes back after months away, I never know whether on that first glimpse I will adore him, hate him or feel a tide of indifference wash over me. More to the point, will I recognise the reasons I chose to be with him? Human feelings are complex and anarchic. They float up from murky depths, where unfulfilled dreams, forgotten talents, and unbearable memories live, and where every second of our sentient history is filed and ready, at some signal we don't even know we are giving, to flood our presence and either overwhelm us with pain, or transport us to greater rapture.

Whatever way we look at it, being apart for months on end is a pain. Absence does not make the heart grow fonder; all it does is stop daily irritations developing while putting the heart on hold. It is our winter, the roots of our relationship are there but there is not much growth. All the same, right from the start we have written every day, protracted one-sided conversations about what we're doing and feeling, keeping each other up to date, so we don't spend all leave wondering what the other is talking about. (There's no e-mail on here.)

And I keep H in touch with island life, wild rather than human, although both are interesting, describing the otters, seals, ducks and birds we share our lives with, telling him when and whether they are breeding, and how many young have survived the serially killing mink. Also, whether the *ménage à trois* of swans, Bill, Isa and Phyllis, are still visiting the septic tank feeding station and consuming mountains of brown bread. And whether Bill is mating with both Isa and Phyllis (as we have seen him do and not withdrawn his rations), and despite all that stuff about swans mating for life and being an example to us all. I tell him, too, about the bullocks that plod about our 70-acre croft, enjoying possibly the best years of their short lives.

Unfortunately, writing is not the ramshackle, unpredictable affair life is. The opposite, in fact. Writing polishes and tidies, rearranges and stylises and, at the end of the day, it is just not enough.

But for months on end it's all we've got, and when H comes home, and we move again, he from his captain's I-take-no-nonsense role, and me from my singleton-and-happy-to-be-so role, and put on our partners' clobber, our time together has to compete with a backlog of domestic chores and schemes, which continuous couples do in their evenings and weekends. Then there is the seeing friends and family, and running the home, garden and croft, all of which means that the seventeen days he earns for every month at sea passes in a flash.

The truly horrible part of reunions is that, no sooner has being together become normal again, than we start wondering how on earth we are going to endure another brutal parting, and trying not to think about it, let alone mention it. But it's there. For every second of every leave, it's there in our dislocated, stop-start life. And, while I know we have a privileged existence compared to most people on the planet, I do not use the abysmal lot of others to ignore the effects of this dislocation, but try instead to diminish its impact.

Being at sea together is great for both of us, and if I did not trail, we would be apart for eight months out of twelve.

I know the electrician feels his separation from his family keenly, as many seamen do. His woes have been added to, as he has hit his head on a cast iron beam. 'It's okay,' he says from the corner barstool, where he sits every evening before dinner, nursing one Coca-Cola and smoking roll-ups. 'No problem. I don't need doctor in Belgium.'

H is not so sure. 'You should get it checked out; you could have delayed concussion or there could be problems later. If you don't see a doctor, you'll get no compensation.' Even if H were not concerned, he would have to say all that to cover himself.

'Sure I be dizzy,' he admits, 'but head is hard from football,' and he clonks it and winces. 'I was professional in Croatia.' I look impressed. 'Yes, really, professional. But I was stupid. A big club wanted to buy me, but I say no, because my contract to small club is not over. But the old club did not give me good money, so I leave anyway. If I stay, I be rich man now!' And he laughs with his characteristic shrug, his eyes, like Eeyore's, gloomy at the edges. 'And I be home!' he adds 'Home!' and he shuffles off in front of us to the saloon, his head bent to the right, his body saying what is the point of poking about with wires all day, miles from home, missing everyone.

Once again, we are being pushed about by a mean to vicious swell shrouded in what looks like a scratchy grey blanket. Our small circle of sea is the colour of washed-out Wedgwood, and up north, according to one report, severe storms are giving thirty-six foot waves. Rolling is moderate most of the time, but every now and again, there is a winter Atlantic special. At breakfast, one of these threw a bowl of rice into the air, the grains falling like droplets from a fountain. Juan dived to his knees apologising, grabbing at crockery, cutlery, rice and toast floating idly about in a river of table water. From the galley below came the sound of a plate fight.

The rolling doesn't slow us down; the opposite if anything, which H says is worse as we'll get there early. I move back to the heavy weather workstation A (the lounge) and jam myself in for the day. When the lecky comes up for smoko, he says I should have stayed in workstation C—bed—

which is where he feels like going. His head is woolly and he has had no sleep. 'But no doctor. Don't need doctor,' he adds quickly, as though I am about to insist.

By midday, the moderately-confused sea is demented and we are pitching, rolling and, in between, almost stopping, like a fazed horse refusing a jump. A second swell dead ahead has joined the one on the port beam, and a mountain of spray is covering the deck from the fo'c'sle to the stern, sometimes ballooning in slow motion, sometimes forming a lacy white curtain that spreads as it falls. Deck work is impossible and time is running out for the crew to get the ship looking spruce for Zeebrugge. It's hard on this run in winter; there is never enough dry weather, but the chief officer had hoped for a day or two for washing down. Nobody wants to arrive in port with tears of rust all over the hull and salt-caked decks.

With work impossible outside, the men start to paint the inside of the accommodation windows, painting ours first which means we have to decamp to the owner's suite next door. Paint is a migraine trigger for me, but maritime paint is lethal. From great distances it makes me gag; close up and I'm a cot case.

In the evening, as we are falling all over the cabin trying to dress for dinner, Eduardo, one of the crew leaving, calls to invite us to his birthday party. 'Thank you,' someone using my voice says brightly, 'We'd love to come.' So after dinner, off we go.

The entire crew bar gets to its feet when we go in and they thoughtfully clear seats for us in front of the monster television. At full volume, a mooning, lovely young woman, with flowing black hair and dreamy lakes for eyes, is just about to collapse in the arms of a wound-up plastic, well-corseted man, with luminously slicked-down hair and a glue-on grin. It is impossible to escape.

'What was your last ship?' I ask the oiler to my left when the music dies.

'The *QE2*, Ma'am,' he says—as quick as a flash—as though he has been waiting for the question all trip. 'I was on when she went aground.' This is a piece of luck. More than light relief.

'Were you down below?'

'No, Ma'am, I was a utility hand. I was collecting dishes in the dining room.'

Better still. 'What happened? Did you feel anything?'

'Everyone felt it, Ma'am. There was a big jerk and the ship stopped. But it was really strange. No one moved. They just went on eating, Ma'am.

They were very British,' and about ten Filipinos fall about me clutching their sides, uncontrollable at the very idea of a dining room full of people with no sense of self-preservation.

'Surely some of them must have stopped eating?' I say, in profound disbelief. 'They can't all have been very British!' More hysterical side-clutching.

'Well, some looked surprised, Ma'am, and raised their eyebrows and stopped eating for a short time, but then the dining room manager came in and said that there had been a hitch, but there was nothing to worry about and, after that, nobody seemed worried.' A hitch is such a handy word but hardly adequate for a dead stop at sea. Ships don't stop suddenly unless they hit something. And even an emergency stop, which cuts the revs and is very bad for the engine, will only slow a ship down gradually. 'It was amazing, Ma'am. The people were so calm and about half an hour later the captain came on the loud speaker and said the same, that there was a hitch but there was nothing to worry about.'

'Amazing!' we all say, clinging hard to the black leatherette to avoid sliding into each other's arms as the ship takes another huge roll. When we are upright again, I say, 'I'm sure you didn't roll like this.'

'Yes, Ma'am, we did,' he says quickly, 'we rolled a lot. There are stabilisers, but she goes very fast, about 24 knots, and often we pitched and pounded as bad as on here, especially going to New York and lots of the passengers were often in the hospital having seasick injections, it was so bad.' And once more, they all collapse into paroxysms at the passengers' expense, and I laugh too, even though I know that death is preferable to seasickness, and to have paid through the nose to spend your days in the hospital throwing up and being injected seems extreme misfortune.

I blame the blatantly false image of the word 'cruise'. No one hears it and thinks storms, throwing up, endless clinging to fixtures, let alone incineration, hurricanes, sudden stops on rocks or taking to the boats. Yet these are not rarities. With a huge crew, any one of whom may smoke carelessly, and any number of passengers making toast in their quarters etc., well, I rest my case.

Still, no matter what the evidence, 'cruise' will always mean silky seas, balmy starlit nights, plenty of deckchairs, and no intruding camcorders or fighting for rail space in the Panama Canal. 'Cruise' has also managed quite spuriously to acquire a reputation for nurturing romances, pretending to be the venue where embarrassingly rich men in faultless toupees and women in wigs, politely sweep each other off their feet at tea dances. Say cruise and you don't think boatloads of bores and drunks slobbering inconsiderately, or of being buttonholed by bigots, or stalked by the deranged. To hear the word is not to think Jed.

Yet even in my limited experience of freighter passengers, who like to think of themselves as the no nonsense end of the market, I've sailed with one morose mutterer who hated all the other passengers and fired vituperative barbs at them at every meal. Another who always introduced himself as Bert—B-E-R-T—spelling it out so slowly we were mystified and highly amused. Then there were the two who left improving tracts down the backs of chairs, while several, who had been everywhere and could speak of nothing else, bored us silly and assumed we hadn't been anywhere. Yet another was particularly annoying as he ate an entire jar of Rose's marmalade every morning, forcing H to go without. Clearly, he feared scurvy.

And there was one seriously deranged bruiser of a man, who came on board without the medication that kept him on bland, and took against the captain so badly he tried to have him sacked, and he would have run amok had he not been drunk most of the time. Or so said the doctor who finally had him taken off the ship in the interest of everyone's safety.

Every now and again, the music makes talking impossible, especially when Eduardo, the birthday boy, has first go on the karaoke and pumps himself up for the high notes, and misses. Talented Ernesto follows him patiently from key to key. 'Smohohke ... smoke gets in your eyes,' he wails just under the note. It certainly does, and your lungs, your hair, your clothes and the pores of your skin.

'There were over a thousand crew, Ma'am,' the Oiler continues, during a break in this painful wail. 'Mostly British, but there were three hundred Filipinos and some Filipinas and we slept four to a cabin.'

The break isn't long. 'Seddy had to work, so I went to the show alone,' croaks Eduardo in his best croon, 'turned down the lights and turned the projector on, then when the news of the world started to begin, I saw my baby and my best friend waaaaaalk in.' They love this. They love screeching to the tear-jerking chorus, 'Saahad movies always make me cry eye eye eye Saahahad movies ...'

'Do people like working on the *QE2*?'

'Not me, Ma'am,' he says without hesitating, 'it's much better on here. Much better. There, we worked twelve hours a day and often we didn't see daylight for days if we were down below washing up. And after work we slept. And six to a cabin is awful after being on these ships.'

The crew quarters here are good. They all have their own cabins, of course, with a desk, a settee and a separate bathroom, which was the norm at one time. Today, with all costs being cut, it's common for new ships to have communal washrooms for the crew and reduced quarters with small windows for officers. And while the captain had a suite with a bedroom, a dayroom and an office, that's no longer the case. The irony is that unions fought for years for conditions which made people feel valued and which are now being eroded as though the fight had never taken place. And the unions are certainly not doing anything about it.

'I think they take advantage of Ernesto,' I say to H when we get back to camping out in the owners' suite. 'A party is just another place to order him about.'

The owners' suite isn't as homely as ours, or as tatty. But then it isn't used much. And never by owners. When the ship was built, owners sometimes travelled around the coast or even across the pond, to see 'how she handled, and was bearing up.' Or they sent one of their extra sons on the equivalent of work experience.

But they can't have enjoyed it. The twin beds are only as wide as hammocks, but not as comfortable or safe, and without the comfort and stabilising effect of the marital cling, we have to use all our energy not to fall out during the bigger rolls. Sleep is impossible in the beds, so we drag the mattresses onto the deck and jam our feet against the bulkhead to stop shooting out feet first, and at our heads we make a barricade with a few chairs. It doesn't work. With each roll, the chairs slide a bit further away, and we slide with them, which is probably just as well. Being catapulted out headfirst is one thing, but colliding with a chair leg every few minutes is no fun, and may soon add concussion to the sizeable list of perils.

By morning, I am so tired I stay in my makeshift bed reading *To the Lighthouse*, sleepily following the twists and turns of Virginia Woolf's illuminating prose, shining its great and often amusing beacon into the nooks and crannies of her characters' interior landscapes. I love this book and take it everywhere. (I also take Woolf's *The Waves* which, so far, I have never been able to finish, even at sea.) For a while, the book distracts me from the rolling, the smell of paint, the shrouded horizon and the thought of H wave-watching on the bridge. The movement means it is not comfortable anywhere, as we are still at the mercy of two swells.

But ship life goes on and it's time to order the stores, so the office computer is in demand. Everything they need for the next two months has to be ordered in Belgium. When H was the chief officer, he had to order all the paint, rust remover etc. for the deck. Now he's moved up, he's responsible for cabbages, cauliflowers and bread without fingernails. After smoko, he questions the cook and the steward about their strange request for twelve mop heads, peppermint tea bags, an out of control number of black plastic rubbish bins, and gallons of furniture polish. I am yet to learn what they said.

Masters doing the catering is comparatively new. Chief stewards, known as grocers, disappeared quite a while ago. The gravy train they were on suddenly stopped with a jolt and they were obliged to get off and console themselves with their Swiss bank accounts. The job didn't disappear, of course; it was just added to the master's, minus the great scope for fiddling of course. I have learnt all this from that well-known informant, Hearsay, and realise that it will not have been true in all cases. And may be untrue in all cases. I am covering myself here. I don't want threats.

As it happens, H is a brilliant all-round caterer. It was, as I mentioned, his supermarket arms which first caught my eye, as they looked capable of supporting multiple plastic bags without his fingers being severed. What's more, he gave the impression he would not have panic attacks in the white light of oxygen-starved and Musak-filled aisles, and not be fazed by the chore of reading E numbers and searching for non-exploitative lines. And how right I was.

Even today, to see him in command of a trolley is to know again that original destabilising passion, and to congratulate myself for grasping how enduring supermarket arms are. Where others may look for swaggering machismo or sensitive odes to their beauty, I know the irresistibility of the well-rounded caterer. It is the practicalities that count for the long haul. Nothing kills passion faster than having to lug all the shopping home yourself. Supermarket arms are for life. And the most amazing thing is that he likes catering, from the shops to the table. But then, he isn't home often enough for it to become tedious.

Another night of violent pitching, most of which H spends on the bridge. I sleep eventually and when I wake after eight it's still dark but the movement has gone, and I find a little pile of ageing, leathery, buttered toast by the bed and a note hoping I have slept for two. He knows how to quadruple my love.

When I pull the curtains, the sun is rising and sending flames shooting high, making the few wisps of cloud into strands of candyfloss. Above the horizon, a huge angel in cardinal red, with wings erect and skirts fanning out, is playing a trumpet. Angels appear regularly in these massive skies. It's easy to see why they caught on as heralds, guides and general religious factotums. As the morning turns golden, the sun rises quickly over a crushed velvet sea, and I watch the angel fade and completely forget last night's battering and my obsession with last things.

We are approaching the Azores. The high has come at last, and we all go about smiling saying this is the life, tra la la la la. Even the Lecky is happy. His head is still sore and he hasn't slept, but life's good. And as for the sparkie, he's grinning in a very witnessy way. 'God is good,' he reminds me, as I pass the radio room. I smile a born-again smile; I can't resist the pleasure he gets from our witnessing conspiracy. For a moment, I wonder what it's like being swaddled in illusions, and then I remember we all are. But, on the whole, it's not good. It clutters the soul. If you spot them in yourself, they are best challenged.

On deck after lunch, it is still seductively beautiful, with gannets and gulls whirling and squawking about me and two schools of dolphins weaving, splashing and cavorting as only the world's best synchronised swimmers can. One good day at sea is worth a lifetime on land, I think, as *War and Peace* falls unread into my lap. Even the terrifying ones are worth it for this.

In the evening, the sinking sun flings shards of gold onto the wake, and gaudy pink patches daub the velvety navy water reflecting the flaming sky. In no time the whole of our dowdy stern, with its seen-better-days green deck, cream rails, rusty incinerator and functional ropes, is brilliantly transformed until even the lifeboat, golden pink above the deck, looks otherworldly and desirable.

The new moon is still up after dinner, one golden crescent so brilliant that the whole, dull aluminium ball is visible. We stay out for a long time watching the stars popping into the gently swaying blackness. Tiredness finally drives us in.

Even before it's fully light, the grey hills of Tierciera are shapes on the horizon and a short while later Pico and São Jorge drift into view. After sunrise, the mountains of São Miguel are clear and sharp, although we are many miles off. We are on GMT again but there's still an extra hour tonight to put us on continental time for arrival in Marin in Spain.

An extra hour to party. Tonight we have been invited to the party for the off-signing celebrants, as the Filipinos leaving us are grandly described. And there's no getting out of it when you're trailing and the captain likes his men to feel valued. However, knowing I can't face another karaoke-induced trance, H suggests a few distracting games (with prizes) and puts the word out on the galley radio. By lunchtime, there is no other topic. Excitement is on every face.

Every face except the Oiler, who comes to the office to announce portentously that, 'If the third engineer comes to the party, I will have my own celebration. I cannot celebrate with this man.' And he adds that he will be pressing charges in Manila.

'You are free to express your grievance in this way,' says H in his Solomon voice, 'but the celebration is open to everyone. I can't ban the third engineer. He has had his warning.' The oiler is miffed, but accepting, and stays away.

We start with two games of bingo, me calling, and the third officer wins a tube of toothpaste for the top line, which his dentist wife will like he says, and the Second Engineer wins a bottle of Bacardi for the full house, and immediately shares it.

In the beer drinking competition, I disqualify everyone as their glasses are still half-full, and immediately regret it. They repeat the repulsive spectacle without a pause, and the Engine Fitter turns deathly pale, and then green and has to sit down and stare at his trainers. For a while, I worry that his skinny frame and small organs may not be coping with two pints of gas and he may be about to explode, but no, he soon lifts his head, smiles broadly, and starts downing a beaker of Bacardi.

Pass the Parcel is a sensation. They've never played it before, and respond so rapturously that I wonder if H and self might not be naturals for the party games business. I'm in charge of the music and because the prospect of removing a layer of newspaper from a large biscuit tin is so heart-stopping, I make sure every heart is stopped, and no one notices that chance has nothing to do with it. I am even able to make sure that the fourth engineer wins the $5 note lying where the Rover Assorted Creams once were, and although he is delighted, he has to quickly cover his disappointment when he sees that all the biscuits have been eaten long ago.

Unfortunately, they are not happy when the games finish and pester H for more. Our repertoire is exhausted, but someone produces toilet paper and eventually H agrees to let them wrap each other like mummies.

Starting at the feet, the idea is to cover their partners totally without breaking the paper. It's harder than it looks and the lounge ends up littered with toilet paper and, as H can't square this frivolous waste of his catering budget, he offers a prize for anyone who can rewind it as new. Romeo wins hands down, although several of them go at it as though they are hand painting Ming china.

When I ask Romeo how he acquired all these skills, he shrugs shyly and tells me that his mother had wanted him to be a priest (he looks like a priest). 'But I want to get married, Ma'am.'

'Soon? Have you anyone in mind?'

'Yes, Ma'am. If my girlfriend will have me, then maybe next year, maybe later,' and he waggles his hands about and smiles his intelligent smile. 'After I am married, I am going into business with my brother. Probably some transport business in Manila. But first we need the capital.' He sounds confident he will make a living, even a fortune. Commerce and Romeo are made for one another. 'I think I will make the curtains too, Ma'am, and Juan can help. I will show you a sample tomorrow.' I have agreed to act as decor consultant.

The accommodation is cooling down so fast we need extra blankets, as well as vests and sweaters. It's winter again.

When Romeo shows me the curtain, I am astounded at what a tailoring course, a bit of old sheet and two ripped curtains can produce. 'I have made all kinds of clothes, Ma'am, even suits for men and I have done some upholstery, but this is the first time I have made a curtain.' I suggest he go into the lucrative decor market, and wish I hadn't. I wait for him to tell me that that is for effeminate men, as he did when I suggested he take up hairdressing as he cuts everyone's hair. He doesn't, but he gives me a loaded look. I resist the urge to say anything. We both laugh.

Inside and out, the ship is being spruced up. The stairs and passageways are gleaming, the stewards having polished them until we can see ourselves underfoot, and the decks are being washed down with salt and rust remover.

It's too cool to read on deck, so I curl up in the suite and re-read the *The Road from Coorain*, the story of Jill Ker Conway's life on an unimaginably huge sheep station in the outback of Australia. She makes me feel the immensity of the sky, the vastness of the land, the heat, the dryness, the struggle to live in a world bleached by the sun. In Coorain, as at sea, you could not live at one remove from the elements, insulated against their effects, ignorant of your intimate relationship with physical creation. You could not grow up, as I did, lamentably deprived of knowledge of the natural world, while reading books and seeing images of a place called England (not even Britain). Such is the power of colonisation that the astonishing richness and beauty of New Zealand was not to be fully promoted for another generation. And of course religion put the natural world not even second but a resounding last. We were preparing for paradise, not realising we were in it.

How I envy her that early intimacy and love of the earth, that profound and enduring connectedness, which is the basis of all connections human and animal. Not being intimate with your environment, and the forces that shape us all, is a great loss, and hard to make up for later. But the damage is not permanent. We humans, and our amazing brains, can recover from almost all early programming.

'Don't write from here,' says H when he sees me tackling my correspondence, 'Belgium is more reliable.' All the same, I make a start on the great list, feeling a huge need to tell the world what a vicious place the North Atlantic can be in winter. Not that they'll believe me. It is universally believed that I am swanning about, being indulged in every possible way. My protests will be as chaff in the wind. It is just not possible for anyone to imagine two huge swells at once (one on the port beam), or daily being intimate with the Last Things.

FOG AND MARIN

H is called at 2am to cross the busy traffic lanes carrying ships up to Finisterre and the Bay of Biscay, and down to the Mediterranean and all points south. It's hairy in good visibility but, in fog that's as thick as an arctic blanket, it's a nightmare.

When I first become aware of the foghorn I manage to incorporate it into a dream, but I am soon sucked back to consciousness and fly out of bed, tear open the dayroom curtains and see absolutely nothing. Not a hatch, not a bow wave and certainly not the mast light. Instead, we are in a fuzzy cocoon, an eerie, grey-white ethereal cloud with, here and there, circles of bright gold which, I slowly realise, are our lights. It is 0300 and we could be gliding in the heavens.

Seduced and fascinated, I gaze for ages at this shrunken, womblike world which is so embracing it seems impossible to feel alarmed. Eventually I become aware that the dayroom is freezing, so scuttle back and try for more sleep, but it's impossible with the foghorn droning. So from time to time, my restless spirit gets my reluctant body up for another look, trying not to think what a nightmare it is for H (it must be taking years off his life) and hoping we are through the really busy part.

Not long before we reach the entrance to the Ría de Pontevedra that will take us up to the small Spanish port of Marin, I catch glimpses of a black sky bright with scattered gold. Eventually the mast light blinks, the bow wave swishes golden in the ship's lights and we are sailing into an exquisite world with excellent visibility.

H has no more sleep. Normally, he would get his head down for an hour or so between the lanes and the entrance to the Pontevedra, but in fog he has to be on the bridge all the time. I sleep eventually, and know nothing about the slow wash up the river to Marin until I start thrashing about as though being suffocated and come to retching and panicking with the most hideous smell creeping into my nostrils, my mouth and my lungs. I am mystified, as it is too repulsive to be galley smells. I hold my nose, gulp through my mouth and crawl under the blankets, hoping it will be gone before I need air again. Then I remember. It is La Celulosa—the paper factory—and that the wind must be blowing the fumes our way. But worse: it is making me relive my worst ever smell trauma I thought I'd buried.

It happened in Bombay. I was alone in a downmarket hotel room—really a cubbyhole—in a large house whose grand rooms had been partitioned by cardboard which swayed if I accidentally touched it when I moved in my extremely narrow bed. I was happy. It had not yet occurred to me to wish I were round the corner in the comfort of the 5-star Taj Mahal.

Next door, close enough for me to touch them, four men were playing cards, while keeping me awake with their continuous wheezing, coughing and farting. They all had chronic catarrh, and even routine breathing and swallowing sounded like heaving and gulping.

Eventually, with the help of earplugs, I slept, only to be woken by a repulsive smell.

To escape, I jammed things up my nostrils, gagged my mouth and crawled to the end of the bed. It was no use; even with used socks up my nose, I could smell it. Sickly, sweet and powerful enough to kill, I knew I was not going to get used to it.

By now, it was three in the morning and, because I was desperate, I went to reception, which was a small boy in grubby rags, asleep on the front doormat. When I had prodded him awake, I begged him to look into it. He sniffed the air curiously and had no idea what I was on about, which was sad in itself, but too much for me to take on board. Back in my partition, the smell was worse.

Twice more I got up and begged anyone I could find to investigate. The third time, I was bundled unceremoniously into my room by a hostile man muttering 'a young man—one of you—rotting'. He also said 'police,' 'drugs,' and 'statement' and finally, 'you must be staying put in your room,' while wagging his finger at me. As soon as his back was turned, I was out the door—fortunately he didn't lock it—and up the eerie early morning Bombay street just seconds before the police arrived. Sitting on the wall near the Gateway, thinking how wonderful it would be to be tucked up in the Taj, it came to me that he clearly thought the unfortunate a brother to me in some real or seedy way, and that I too was a junkie (if indeed he was). Just being in a hotel alone meant that I was a prostitute, or that I was hawking whisky and other duty frees to finance my loafing about the subcontinent in search of my lost spiritual self.

All of this was so wide of the mark—I was there for an intensive yoga course at the Iyengar Institute in Pune—but that smell of putrefying flesh will be forever in my memory and instantly recallable.

Fortunately, the smell of Marin is not putrefying flesh, but it is still hard to endure and has cast a blight on the town. Don't linger here, say all the guidebooks. I only live here because I have to, say the residents. And one of the first things you see as you sail in is a smart-looking school on a promontory overlooking the harbour, which has been deserted by pupils, teachers and the birds in the trees because, when the wind is in the wrong direction, the smell is unbearable.

Out on deck, I am just in time to see the good-looking pilot gracefully scaling the pilot ladder, the ship's lights showing up his satiny olive skin, a touch of grey at the temples of an otherwise dark head, and his pleasingly-arranged features. On the bridge, his very serious face opens like an interesting book when he smiles. We are just outside the town near a large rock or small island, the Isla Tambo, where a lovely spiral lighthouse sits in front of an unlovely cash crop of eucalypts. It's a short pilotage (about five minutes), but in that time he tells me that he used to live in Vigo but has moved to Marin *only*, he stresses the 'only' and shrugs winsomely, so he can go home between ships. But of course, he doesn't like it, which is the near universal verdict on the fishing village/tourist town turned purpose-built banana port. And it is certainly the smell that has blighted it.

Like Santa Marta, Marin looks pretty from the sea. It lies near the head of the Ría de Pontevedra and the small port is lolling with fishing boats and a not unattractive naval college building just across from our berth. It's still early and not fully light as the linesmen tie us up, but the dock is deserted. There is a new-looking cream and red functional banana shed on the quay, and several conveyor belts are standing ready to take the boxes straight from the ship's side. It's a quick and clean operation, so doesn't take long.

Around ten, we go ashore together in the agent's Fiat. Uniformed police with dogs are sniffing about the conveyor belts and a few supervisors in navy anoraks are walking about, sometimes jumping or throwing their arms about to keep warm. Near the gate, we pass great pallets of logs. 'From Brazil,' says the agent, 'they have cut down the rainforest so they can grow this stuff. It's an ecological disaster there and now they want to do the same here.' In his excellent English, he tells us that he is both a botanist and an entomologist and that this is making him very sad. 'That island,' he says, pointing to Tambo, 'is full of particularly destructive eucalypts. There is a great fight going on here between the economists and the environmentalists. They want to do what they have done in Brazil and destroy a rainforest so they can grow eucalypts.' We sigh in solidarity. A sigh full of green credentials.

Marin is really a fishing town, although a wander through the fish market doesn't show to what extent this part of Galicia is dependent on the sea because the big market is in Pontevedra (the provincial capital), and a lot of people catch their own. But, says the agent, the sea is Marin's lifeblood; most people's jobs are connected with it directly or indirectly. 'Apart from the wood,' he mutters. 'In the summer, many people from the rest of Spain are here. You can't move. Outside Marin there are many beaches and also on the other side,' and he waves his hand across the water at the Peninsula de Salnés where cream houses with terracotta roofs huddle attractively behind smiling semicircles of sand.

'And where do people from Marin have their holidays?'

'In the summer, they stay here because that is when they are very busy.'

'And you?'

'Me?' He laughs. 'When I have my holidays I get as far from the sea as I can. This year, I will be going to the Pyrenees and I will be sitting under a tree and reading a book. I have enough of the sea. And of cities.'

'You don't fancy a cruise, then?' says H, the wag.

It's good to get ashore, even for a couple of hours. And even better to walk. After H has dialled his various paymasters from the agent's office (which is only a small branch—the real thing is in Vigo), and I have waited outside to avoid the cigarette smoke billowing around the two-desk room, we walk the camellia-lined road to town. The pavement is badly potholed with building sites everywhere. And most buildings are concrete and ugly and look as though they have been put up in a great hurry and are ageing gracelessly. Even the older stone ones nearer the centre are falling into a charmless decay and in places vegetation is insinuating itself around anything that will have it, and leafy stems are forcing their way through cracks. Wrought iron adds interest in places, but it doesn't manage to make the decay appear quaint or the shoddiness charming.

'Winter is not the time to see Marin,' says a short, stout, dark-haired woman—the perfect genes for the climate. She shakes her head and looks at us hard. 'It's a shame to come now and Monday is not good either,' and she deposits *two café con leche (grande)* and folds her arms. 'Are you from Eng-eeland?' She doesn't smile, but the folds about her eyes soften. Marin is not a place of smilers or surplus words or gestures.

'Scotland,' we chorus. Several heads turn any one of which could have been Scottish, were it not for the black berets and the fact that their squat persons are perched on high stools at the bar sucking on fags. They are all drinking tiny cups of strong coffee and once they have decided we are not just harmless but dull they go back to their large newspapers, or return to gazing into the middle distance.

'Do you know Guilford?' she asks.

'Yes,' meaning I have been there.

'I am many years in Guilford in a lingerie shop.' She sucks her lips in, presses them together and out again, like a primitive sea creature.

'Very nice place, Guilford.'

I try to think of something to say about it—the cathedral, a theatre, near Box Hill, which I once had to climb on a school trip with 4C, and discovered vertigo and school trip phobia. But the memory which nudges all these aside is of two perfectly synchronised teaching colleagues who swept in every morning and one spent the day teaching history—drumming it in was her phrase—and the other maths before they set off again from Bethnal Green to Guilford.

Between their two journeys, they glided about as though they had wind-assisted passage, or she did and he sailed in her wake, and she had a classroom next to mine where the only sound was of pins dropping. All day. She was a stranger to both self–and curricular–doubt, and knew nothing of moral murk. Or so I thought, until one Friday afternoon when she threw open the staff room, sailed up to the desk where I was marking O Level questions on *Twelfth Night*, and demanded to know whether I had ever done anything morally reprehensible. Or to be exact whether I thought I had. Morally reprehensible! It was almost too big to contemplate and made mortal sin sound flighty.

I've no idea what I said. It certainly wasn't 'yes', or 'give me an example', or 'have you', or 'eff off, you harlot'. Whatever it was, it certainly was not enough to stop me wondering to this day whether she thought I had, what it meant, or whether she was trying to tell me she suspected me of letting 5A1 discuss sex/contraception/the bomb/communism or all four for a double period on a Friday afternoon.

That aside, in Marin I enthuse about Guilford and ask why Monday is the wrong time to be here.

'The market. The market is on Tuesday or Thursday but really, the summer is best for visiting, after Easter, I'd say. We have wonderful beaches, and many people come from Madrid and everywhere in Spain, and then the shops will be open. Now, many shops, they are closed for the winter.' She says all this rather sadly, as though she is talking to two of life's losers. And she shakes her head, 'Now it is not so good. It is …' she looks out the café window and rakes the street with her eyes, as though hoping to alight on the word, and suddenly looks back and says, 'dead. Marin is dead now.' The word drops like a stone between us and she smiles the smile of one who has hit the nail on the head to her complete surprise, and then does her mollusc mouth again.

When afterwards we walk about the town, rather taken by this dead, totally unpretentious place, there is not a poser in sight; the winter people of Marin do not have an image or attitude problem. They are not what the world would call beautiful, but neither are they self-conscious. Well-turned-out young women in neat jeans and leather jackets wheel cosy-looking prams, and older ones bustle about, their arms either folded against the cold or clutching large wicker baskets. Sometimes, two of them are so deep in conversation, their pale faces are almost touching and their baskets are protruding from their hips while Marin flows about them.

Of the men, the younger ones make brief, brisk appearances, clutching small leather handbags with a preoccupied air. I mustn't drop this, their hands say; whatever happens, I must clutch this bag. This bag is me; I am this bag, and they rush down narrow hole-like side-streets like the White Rabbit. The older men, in stark contrast, sit still as statues on the white wooden benches lining the paved, tree-lined park in the town centre. They appear to have taken root. Only their heads move occasionally as they follow, with empty eyes, an old woman in black who taps her way across the road, into the park, past their seats and up into a narrow steep street behind. Her red plastic shopping bag flaps at her side and her old bent legs look tired and veiny as she scans the ground, taking care to keep to her path. Occasionally, a couple stroll by, clinging to one another as though joined at the hip. Mostly, though, whether in the café, the market or the street, the genders do not mix.

41 Winter time, Marin

The main road is busy; most of the traffic is passing through, but a procession of buses from Pontevedra stops frequently, and a tide of workers looking hurriedly turned-out, harassed and not awfully well—as though they have smoked one fag too many and are longing for the spring to warm their damp bones—washes across the busy road and disappears into the town, leaving the scene as before.

'It reminds me of Oban,' I say, thinking the same genes are common, and where people talk in the street while the world passes round them and, most particularly, where you see proud young women with serious-looking prams and an admiring island of aspiring pram pushers. Young women advertising the joy of motherhood with everything still freshly frilled, basking in their enviable status, and not yet ground down by terrible twos and part-time fathers. And without that why-didn't-someone-tell-me-it-would-be-like-this look. 'I know Oban doesn't have older women in black and is much busier in the winter.'

Under the recently restored band rotunda, I gaze at the lovely wooden roof with its fringe of wrought iron pretending to have no idea that H is snapping me. Earlier, I've sat outside the café and gazed into the middle-distance to produce the same effect. I am trying to fulfil a lifelong desire: a need, if I'm honest, to look as though I am having deep thoughts. I fail every time. Around me, gulls and feral pigeons strut in thuggish packs, and in the compartmentalised gardens, rows of heavily pruned hydrangeas and standard roses are surrounded by low, spindly hedges. Two rows of tall bare trees arch high over the old men on the benches.

Just beyond the gardens, a woman with sleeves rolled up and spit on her duster is violently polishing the stainless steel counter of her kiosk. Spit, rub, spit, rub she goes, looking at it from all angles and in all lights. When she suspects a smear, she's on it, elbow up, head down. 'Out, damned spot,' say her frantic arms. Out. Out. Spit, rub, spit, rub. Finally, when she is sure not a smear can be seen in any light, she gets inside the small space, pulls down her sleeves, sits and fluffs out her feathers, and lights up. She is ready for business and I feel like applauding.

When we wander into the fish market, the bright, white, tiled walls lined with tiled counters are newly-washed and the short, stout women in white aprons and large plastic gloves are sitting silently beneath huge hanging scales. In front of them on marble slabs, shiny silvery fish are looped over one another as though they are still gliding through the water, or they would be if they still had their heads. Pink and fleshy fish lie with green, scaly, mean-looking brutes, and titchy things are curled up as though asleep.

The only windows are high and opaque, throwing a muted light on the freshly-hosed concrete floors. It's not busy; most of the women sit very still, their plump arms folded over their ample bodies and casting only the occasional remark at a neighbour. Sometimes one stands, pulls on long, plastic sleeves and rearranges her display. As we pass, their eyes narrow and follow us with more than a hint of suspicion. They know our sort.

In the narrow steep alleys behind the town's facade, front doors and common entrances to flats open onto narrow pavements. Some have been smartened up with shiny tiling and plants in multi-coloured pots that balance precariously on windowsills. Mangy curs slink about, their mess underfoot. On the gaping windowsills of abandoned houses, gangs of pigeons sit cooing and chuckling, or fly in and out noisily. Where houses are being renovated, concrete mixers and heaps of sand and rubble block the pavement. Washing is strung up everywhere, and I almost wade into a pile of fresh vomit.

One street back from the front, among the small lingerie, knitwear or hardware shops, are many selling the sort of shoes which look as though they may make love to one's feet. Like an alcoholic who thinks one drink will do no harm, I wander nonchalantly into the last one, having resisted the rest.

It's empty. Behind a glass partition, a young woman is lounging easily, talking on the phone. The men's shelves are full of elegant, classy shoes in glowing mahoganies and subtle browns. At this point, I should have left. But seduced, I pull on pair after pair and gaze adoringly, imagining I have died and been reborn in a world where feet were not just feet, but the bigger the better. Seeing me, the young woman whispers to her caller and comes running to point out that these are for *hombres*. (She's first checked that I am not an *hombre*—discreetly—she thinks.)

'Unisex surely,' I suggest, for, even though the word is as lifeless as Carnaby Street, it still does the job in foreign parts which cannot be said for many of my words. But it doesn't quite work here. She pushes her deep red glossy lips out so far she looks like a shelduck in breeding condition, and when she shakes her head as well, I give the game away and admit to needing *cuarenta y tres*.

Unfortunately, she is not ready for this. As she falls back senseless against the mounted tassels, knocking a few askew, her lips come in and her eyebrows knit and her eyes open so wide she resembles a traumatised owl. For a moment, I wish I had done a first aid course. What happens to such persons when they are really shocked? What gestures and expressions do they have in reserve for a dire emergency, when a customer with perfectly normal if exquisite feet, throws them into shock? Feet, in my case, which were once featured in *Here's Health*, demonstrating how to make feet more intelligent and supportive understandings. And I mention this so you know it's not just my opinion and that of my adoring H, but the entire editorial staff of a national health magazine.

I walk away. She follows, alternately gaping and whistling in disbelief, and telling me that no one in Spain has *cuarenta y tres*. 'Never. Never.' More whistling and phews. 'Ziss is so grandez. Zo grandez,' and she looks at my lovelies, which fit the bottom of my legs to perfection, and makes *grande* sizes in the air while whistling and shaking her mop of black hair which I had thought rather pleasant, but which I now see is a literal mop which would clean a floor very nicely, and only tacky rivers of hairspray are keeping it from gorgonhood.

'Any luck?' says H, mooching about in the now utterly slimy alley.

'There were so many I couldn't decide, but it didn't come to that. I got the circus bit. The whistling and phews and the '*grande, grande*', but without the hand-stroking, so I didn't cry. But I did put her in her place.'

'Oh!' H is agog, but playing down his admiration. 'How?'

'She spoke a bit of English, so I grabbed her shell suit, threw her against the wall and said, 'Button it. Button it fast.'

'And did she?'

'Naturally, but then she started to grovel, so I said I hadn't come to Slimesville to listen to some shrink-wrapped walnut brain insulting my lovelies.'

'That was telling her.'

'Yeah. I didn't mention *Here's Health*, but I think she understood, especially when I threw all the shoes all over the shop and told her to stand on her inadequates, if they would hold her, and get it cleared up. Smartish.

'How did that go down?'

'Fine. She saw I meant business, and who was boss, and what side her bread was buttered on etc, and when she stopped blubbering and pulled herself together, I told her there were no hard feelings, and that it wouldn't go any further, and then we exchanged cards, and I said anytime she was in Scotland to come and stay and bring her extended, inadequately-cloven family, and always to remember that you don't sell shoes by insulting your customers, and she thanked me for a wonderful lesson thoroughly learnt.'

'She won't make that mistake again.'

'I hope not. But oh, it takes it out of me throwing things about in shops.' And, I think, not for the first time, that coming ashore is overrated. Compared to the violence of human relating, the harsh, plain-speaking elements are as nothing. Even two swells at once and one on the port beam. Heavy sigh.

When we sail at 13.30, the wind has moved around, taking the noxious fumes with it. As we swish through the silken sea, slowly at first to avoid the many fishing boats and one troublesome rock, a wintry sun in a cloudless sky makes it feel like a cruise. Gannets, gulls, shags and dolphins follow us past a string of pretty cream and terracotta villages, sandy beaches and bays, and endless coves and inlets. Only the steel cages of the many mussel farms, which look like the tops of sinking merry-go-rounds, detract a little.

It's pleasant on deck, but near punkish-looking Isla de Ons, a flat-topped island which is bald except for one tuft of trees and a lighthouse, clouds bubble up and cover the sun. And in the Boca del Sudoeste, where we meet all the tonnage going to and from Vigo and which eventually takes us back to the shipping lanes for Finisterre and the Bay of Biscay, H gets that foggy look. From now on, until we get the pilot at Wandelaar, he will have that shadow over his attention that will pass off as soon as we are tied up, and he says 'at least we didn't have fog.'

I have, of course, often asked him which of the following he would rather never have again, if I could order it: pitching, pounding, rolling and corkscrewing simultaneously; a ruptured tank gushing oil on the bananas; the fridge plant collapsing and all greens going yellow; a suspended pilotage at Wandelaar and his having to take the ship in through the breakwaters with several violent stowaways; being arrested in Spain after drugs found under the grating; or fog in the Channel.

'Fog in the Channel. No contest.' And this from a man who has been treated like something less than a worm by the Spanish authorities who, having been tipped off by some drug grass in far away and high up Madrid, were waiting for him on the quay in Marin, disguised as minibuses. I, unfortunately, was not there at the time to share the opprobrium (as agreed in the marriage vows), or to lend credibility (like it or not, a man with a wife has more; it's not the wife, it's the possession of same, and sexuality not being under suspicion). In foreign ports, you run the gauntlet of every country's particular prejudices.

H was magnificent, as I am sure I do not need to say. With moderate to fast sweet-talking, conciliatory gestures, toad-like co-operation and a saint-like concern for his crew, he got the vessel out of that scrape and on its way. But not before they had all been locked in the saloon, denied food and lavatories, and stared at for several hours by hostile guards who clearly thought them vermin. Further, they were constantly asked, 'Where are ze drugs?' in a tone which assumed they all had brown paper parcels heavily-covered in parcel tape concealed about their cabins.

They searched all cabins, including H's, and it was difficult, he said, not to worry that the dogs would get excited about the void space under the bunk, where stowaways had been known to hide. And he feared something could have been planted in one of the cupboards he'd never even opened because it was full of the last master's old shoes and Meccano, plus the ship's Ludo, snakes and ladders, and scrolled Neptune certificates from the days when anyone had time to play Ludo or to notice they were crossing the line. They even searched his cabin safe and pulled out all the ice-cream cartons full of photocopied money used for change at the horse races, which H tried to explain in his non-existent Spanish by pseudo-galloping. Like most people whose only other language is Gaelic and who are often in foreign countries, he is resourceful.

While all this was going on, and they were intimating that the future was looking grim for him and his ship, and that he would not be going any further for a long time, H could only think about how I would respond to hearing, 'I'm very sorry, but your husband has been arrested in Spain and taken to Madrid where he will be staying until his case comes up which could be well … anytime. I'm very sorry,' they might add.

While I know ships' masters do have to carry the strangest cans, I will still be greatly un-thrilled by this news, but have assured H I will almost certainly throw myself into a 'Free the Lismore One' campaign. And the world will sit up very straight and pay attention as I paint a picture of simple innocence impaled on despicable injustice.

And when I have succeeded in exonerating him, he will not just be free he will be lionised. Lecture tours, *Any Questions*, supermarket openings, and fêtes will all want him, and at the mere mention of 'drug traffic' and 'shipping', the radio car will be on the ferry and every word he utters will be dripping with the unimpeachability of the 'been theres'. Never again will he be ignored; even his silence will signify, as only that of those who have once been truly listened to does.

On the other hand, I may do nothing. One never knows beforehand. But it is not an unknown scenario. And we both wondered what they would have done with me, had I been there.

Fortunately, it didn't come to this. They finally let the ship sail very late, but not without locking up a hold and refusing to have it opened except by the customs in Zeebrugge where, after discharge, the drugs were found under a grating and everyone lived happily ever after. Well, we did for the time being, though no doubt the Cali cartel had something unpleasant to say to someone.

HOME?

Another night of relentless rolling with a three-metre swell, and a force-nine on the port beam. Nothing stays where it is supposed to, which includes H and self in bed, water in hand basin, and breakfast in digestive system. But by now you know all about the unacceptable face of the banana.

To make matters worse, the steam heating is on, which would be good were the crew not still painting indoors. So, to beat bouts of rising nausea, I spend my morning rushing outside to gulp fresh air and rushing back in before the bitter wind blows me overboard or I catch sight of passing vessels completely awash and disappearing into huge waves. Which is exactly what we are doing.

Between times, I sit as still as possible, gaze straight ahead, breathe deeply and calmly consider the pros and cons of continuing. Once or twice, I get my cases out and almost immediately think better of it. It wouldn't do H any good to see them—and we are all relying on him to get us there—all being the ship's company, the owners, the charterers, the management companies (three), the banana importers, conveyors, retailers and consumers (you).

The paint fumes are particularly significant because, having chronic migraines I am delightfully smell-sensitive. Paint fumes anywhere are a trigger too far. On a rolling banana boat in winter, they are pain on a plate. Enough said. One day I may write *Finger on the Triggers*, and expose the whole seedy world of migraines, with their auras, darkened rooms, plastic buckets and drugs to die from.

Late morning, I haul myself up to the see-sawing bridge where the third officer is either struggling up hill, his head bent, on the way to one radar, or running down, his chin in the air towards the other radar. Occasionally he stands, his legs wide, and rakes the heaving sea with the binoculars. From the chart, I see we are passing the mouth of the Loire. Outside, in the draughts created by the force 9, small northern gulls are racing about, slicing through the air or swooping and diving balletically, like surfers riding exhilarating currents. They have been with us on and off since the Azores.

The third officer has The Channels. Everyone going on leave gets them and becomes talkative, punch drunk or generally unfocussed at the thought of land, home and freedom, the name dating from the days when coming home meant sailing up the English Channel. 'I hate to be kept waiting,' he bursts out when I ask what time we will be at Ushant. I wonder if he has heard, and repeat the question; in theory, at least, I am still interested in Ushant. But third officer is thinking about Manila. 'All my life I hate being kept waiting,' he says again, leaning over the chart table and looking straight ahead, as though he is soliloquizing. 'My father never allowed anyone to keep him waiting and I am the same. If I am meeting someone, I do not want to be the one who arrives first. I want to arrive and see them waiting for me.' He reaches for the protractor as though he is still vaguely aware of where he is. Aware that his need to be awaited is not all there is.

Tempted though I am, I don't laugh. I know what he means; returning after a nine-month tour, his control may be diminished, his power withered. It is a vulnerable and exposing time, when the old order is forgotten and may never return. Fortunately, the-one-who-gets-there-first power struggle is not one of our problems. We long ago gave up entertaining the public at airports, bus stations or even the ferry with our version of reunion or departure trauma—they are both as bad as each other for producing impossible to manage emotions. We part and reunite in the house by mutual consent. We have privatised separating. But I fear the third officer's not wanting to be kept waiting is somewhat different, and clearly he is not going to answer my question.

With its many lighthouses and separated traffic lanes, Île d'Ouessant universally known as Ushant in English, is a busy place, which not only marks the beginning of the channel, but is also a control point: at Ushant all ships have to register their tonnage, cargo and next port, and some may even be advised of their onward destination.

I want to know, because I am hoping that once we alter for the Channel, the movement will be less violent. Sadly, it is not. But at least there is no fog, which means that after lunch H lies down hoping to rest, it's far too choppy to sleep. 'Wake me at four,' he says, as he puts on eyeshades and I pull the inadequate curtains. 'I still have a mountain of paperwork before Zeebrugge.' Nothing becomes a mountain faster than paperwork.

At dinner, H hears that the Wandelaar Pilotage has been suspended due to high seas and a frightful forecast and, as this is the stuff of bitten nails, I do not mention that I am dreaming of dry land and Scotland in winter. After dinner, we rock about on the settee (just like the first night), listening to every noise, analysing every roll and trying to pretend we are doing neither, while making conversation as though we are strangers in a supermarket queue. 'It's bound to have blown itself out before we get to Wandelaar,' I say, as we are trying to get ready for bed and H says, 'I think it's better if I keep my trousers on as I'll be up and down ...'

'What happens if the pilotage is suspended?' I ask with feigned indifference. I fool neither myself nor H, who knows perfectly well that I know more about the Wandelaar pilotage than is good for me. But he plays his indifferent role too, stepping into that mined area where he has to select his words so that I am informed, but not so well that I will never walk up a gangway again. 'I might have to go in myself,' he says as though that's nothing.

'Through that small gap in a force 10? I thought you had to know the tides. And that they are treacherous?' He shrugs but doesn't say anything, so I add, 'If masters can take ships in, why do you need pilots?'

'I certainly could do it. I would have to study it and they would give me all the help I needed. This ship is manoeuvrable enough. (Manoeuvrable? This great hulk?) It just depends how bad the weather is. But once the labour and the tugs are booked the cost of cancellation is huge, and the charterers will probably insist I go in.' He smiles one of those have-I-convinced-her smiles. ('If I've convinced her, I have convinced myself.')

'I don't doubt you can do it,' I say, meaning it. H is a very fair judge of his own abilities and has nothing to prove to anyone. 'Why doesn't Belgium get itself a proper pilotage which isn't suspended at the drop of a storm?' I'm not the only one to say or think this; Wandelaar is notorious, not just for its on–off pilotage, but also for the danger of collisions in and around the spot. I cannot go near it without thinking of the tragic collision between the tanker *British Trent* and the bulk carrier *Western Winner*, when nine seafarers died, one a twenty-two-year-old electrician we had sailed with a short time before. Like the rest, he should still be alive. But even without this tragedy, British seafarers have been pushing for improvements at Wandelaar for a long time. When huge ships—or any-sized ships—are picking up or dropping the pilots, they should have plenty of room to manoeuvre, whatever the conditions. And at Wandelaar, dense fog and high seas are not exceptional.

Most pilots come to ships from a land-based station. At Wandelaar, they come in a tiny cutter from a pilot accommodation launch, where they have often slept. When the seas are high and they can't make a lee and get access to the pilot ladder, the pilotage is off. But even in good weather, it can't be a dream job. The launch lurches about and the cutter looks like a suicide mission most of the time. Yet it is a sought-after job, and most of the pilots I have met really like it and seem blissfully unaware of how the rest of us regard the place.

For most of the night, I drift in and out of consciousness, thinking of home. H comes and goes for the Casquets, but there's no improvement. When I finally get up, my red-rimmed eyes smarting and grit-lined, my spirit ragged, ships are pitching and lurching like toys on a stone-coloured boiling sea, and the clumpy buildings of Belgium are sinister shapes hugging the murk-wrapped coast. But oh, how wonderful they look, how stable, how solid and how permanent; proof, as if I needed it, that my spirit is broken. That I have been bananas, I am bananas, and if there is any hope for my stability, I must go home and shun all things boat-shaped and yellow. With glaring clarity, I realise I must go where I can rediscover who I was before the North Atlantic came between me, my banana-carrying partner and sanity. He will have to get the mortgage money alone for the time being. It may not be forever; in time, hopefully pre-retirement, I may forget.

Like a body deprived of bones, I flop onto the bunk and soak the pillow in tears of relief. Then I remember Wandelaar and fly to the window. Ahead, a small tanker, its stern and midships awash, is trying to make a lee and the tiny pilot cutter is making intermittent appearances on the crests of heaving, grey, mountainous waves. So, the pilotage is on, and H will not have to take us in and earn another Sea Scout badge. And neither will he have to cool his heels at the Wandelaar anchorage and miss the banana deadline.

To see the pilot's beatific smile as he rises over the main deck, you would think he had just had the time of his life and not been the equivalent of suspended by an elastic band above a raging torrent. Short and stout, he is neither young nor athletic, and climbs with difficulty, breathing like a bellows. Wisps of reddy-gold hair lash his ruddy face. Wandelaar pilots are seldom young; they have all had sea careers, often as masters, and after training, they don't get ships this size for five years and the really big ones for ten.

'Well, Captain, you may be the last today. Things are getting worse out there,' he says as he plonks his bag on the chart table and starts to remove the many layers of insulation which make him look like the Michelin man. Everyone is smiling at him, but H's smile is warmest. In fact, so much relief and *bonhomie* is flooding the bridge that no one seems to mind the biting wind roaring in one door and out the other. 'And what will happen to the ships with no pilots? Will they go in themselves?' H is still smiling, but he manages to sound nonchalant.

'Today? No. They will all have to anchor. It is too dangerous, even if you know the tides well. They will definitely not be allowed in, Captain.'

So we are the lucky ones. The cargo will get there. The charterer will be happy, no penalty clause will be paid, no heads will roll and shoppers will fill their baskets.

It's about an hour from the pilotage to the breakwater and the storm, if anything gets worse, but the pilot is not fazed. With tiny footsteps, he pads about from bridge wing to radar, standing on tiptoe to peer out, smiling often and calling instructions between drags on his pungent roll-ups. After every command he says 'please', and every response 'thank you', and soon the bridge is reeking of tobacco, and though the air is fuggy, it is also full of his good cheer and politeness.

A P&O ferry goes through the breakwater ahead of us, and inside I notice H pointing and smiling at something. At first, I think he is showing me the umpteen flocks of ducks, or perhaps the amphibious Land Rover driving about, and then I see it too: the ship we met on, at the container berth. It has had a coat of paint, a change of name and new owners, but we would know it anywhere.

For a moment, something of that blissful insanity returns. But melting into each other's arms is not an option. We are not there yet, and even inside the breakwater we are still rolling.

The moment passes quickly, but my rational self knows that this is fate at it again. Just when I most need my cool, fate is making me forget the horrors and believe again that the world is a wonderful place, as long as we are together. But there is no time for romantic reminiscing, and this is not the place.

As we sail into the lock under the huge raised road, gulls scream about on all sides. At the traffic lights, Mr and Mrs Belgium stare impassively from a swaddle of furs as we glide slowly by, and on the towpath, the new crew stand shivering beside their luggage. The roads are full of expensive gliding cars, and a man is head down into the wind, laboriously pedalling his bicycle but making very little progress. All around, Belgium stretches away boringly, yet never did anywhere look more wondrous or more inviting.

The lock pilot is young and so tall and strapping he fills the bridge and almost blocks out the light. When he speaks, his voice booms, resonating in every cavity in his broad chest and generous face, and he inclines his head so that he looks fascinated even to hear one's 'good morning.' He has the softest and kindest eyes, and no sense of his formidable strength. All the same, when he shakes my hand my bones shudder to the shoulder.

'Have you enjoyed your trip?' he booms, smiling.

'Very much,' I say meaning it.

'And how was the weather?'

'Oh … It's been uncomfortable since Marin, but before that it wasn't too bad, really.'

'And is it home to Scotland now?'

'No. This is my first trip. There are three more before I go home.' H looks at me, not sure whether to celebrate or fetch a doctor.

INDEX

ABOUT THE AUTHOR

 Pauline Isabel Dowling was born in New Zealand but moved to London in the early 1970s where she worked briefly as a teacher and then spent five years studying Singing and the Piano at the Guildhall School of Music and Drama. She worked as a freelance writer for a number of London publications and after studying yoga in both London and Pune also became a yoga teacher. She moved first to Dorset and later to the Isle of Lismore on the west coast of Scotland where she worked as a press officer and continued writing and teaching yoga. She has written two previous books: *I Would Like To Have Been A Nun*, her mother's story, and *Reflections of Yoga*, interviews with BKS Iyengar both available, along with her soon to be published poetry, on www.paulinedowling.com.

ABOUT THE BOOK

Did you know that the European Union is the largest consumer of bananas on the planet? Ever wondered where those bananas come from and how they get here? Or what their true price is? Pauline Isabel Dowling found out when she began her unexpected trailing career, which started when she decided to take a ship to New Zealand rather than face another 30-hour ordeal on a long haul flight. That ship was the *ACT 7*, a Blue Star Line container ship, travelling from Tilbury to Auckland. The journey should have taken four weeks, but the ship lost its steering gear in Botany Bay and was tied up in Darling Harbour in Sydney for almost three months, and for much of that time she was the only female on board. It's genetics. It's fate. Whatever it is, she now trails, going to work with her mariner husband like a breathing, talking, additional piece of luggage, challenged daily to be dignified, sane and fulfilled. It's a strange life, not without its merits and certainly not without interest. *My Trailing Career (Volume 1)* describes her first, and last journey on a banana boat, the *MV Avelona Star*.

Printed in Great Britain
by Amazon